The Works of James M. Whitfield

The Works of

JAMES M. WHITFIELD

America

AND OTHER WRITINGS BY A NINETEENTH-

CENTURY AFRICAN AMERICAN POET

EDITED BY

Robert S. Levine & Ivy G. Wilson

The University of North Carolina Press

Chapel Hill

This book was published with the assistance of the Anniversary Endowment Fund of the University of North Carolina Press.

Designed and set in Bembo by Rebecca Evans
Manufactured in the United States of America

The paper in this book meets the guidelines for permanence and durability of the Committee on Production Guidelines for Book Longevity of the Council on Library Resources.

The University of North Carolina Press has been a member of the Green Press Initiative since 2003.

Library of Congress Cataloging-in-Publication Data
Whitfield, James Monroe, 1822–1871.
The works of James M. Whitfield: America and other writings by a nineteenth-century African American poet / edited by Robert S. Levine and Ivy G. Wilson.
p. cm. Includes bibliographical references.
ISBN 978-0-8078-3445-9 (cloth: alk. paper)
ISBN 978-0-8078-7178-2 (pbk.: alk. paper)
1. African Americans—Literary collections. 2. American poetry—African American authors. 3. American poetry—19th century. 4. African Americans—Intellectual life—19th century—Literary collections. I. Levine, Robert S. (Robert Steven), 1953- II. Wilson, Ivy G. III. Whitfield, James Monroe, 1822–1871. America and other poems. IV. Title.
PS3180.W45 2010   818'.309—dc22   2010022656

cloth   15 14 13 12 11   5 4 3 2 1
paper   15 14 13 12 11   5 4 3 2 1

Whitfield commands; your aid, O Muses bring!

What muse for Whitfield can refuse to sing.

—ANON., *Pacific Appeal* (1867)

Contents

PART I *America* 31

PART II Black Nationalism and Emigration 99

PART III Poems from California 205

Acknowledgments

We are pleased to acknowledge the generosity and support of a number of individuals and institutions. We did the bulk of our research and document collecting at the Library of Congress, and we are grateful for the assistance of its expert staff. Our thanks as well to librarians at the Schomburg Center for Research in Black Culture; the Shields Library at the University of California, Davis; the Moorland-Spingarn Research Center at Howard University; and the interlibrary loan divisions of the University of Maryland, the University of Notre Dame, and Northwestern University. For travel and research support, we thank the University of Maryland, the University of Notre Dame, and Northwestern University.

James Holstun provided us with his collection of Whitfieldiana (and his insights about the poetry); Edward Whitley kindly gave us an advance look at his chapter on Whitfield in his *American Bards*; Ezra Greenspan emailed timely information about *America*; and University of Maryland doctoral student Sarah Sillin skillfully assisted with the preparation of texts and annotations. We happily thank them all. A special thanks to Buffalo-based genealogist Ward Bray for providing us with invaluable new information on Whitfield based on his research in various public records, and to Robin Condon and James Hanna at the Frederick Douglass Papers at Indiana University for providing us with copies of two Whitfield poems (a section of "The Vision" and "Lines, Addressed to Mr. and Mrs. J. T. Holly") currently unavailable in the standard microfilm of *Frederick Douglass' Paper*. We are also delighted to thank Kenneth Price and Martha Nell Smith, who helped to give a start to this edition.

At the University of North Carolina Press, we were fortunate to receive engaged responses from the Press's anonymous outside readers. Our warm thanks to those two scholars for helping us to make this into a better edition. Our thanks as well to Beth Lassiter and Stephanie Wenzel for their editorial assistance. Finally, we are happy to thank our editor, Sian Hunter, who saw our edition of *America* grow and grow and never said no. We are grateful now, as we have been over the past several years, for her expert advice and enthusiastic support for our project.

The Works of James M. Whitfield

Introduction

In his own time, James Monroe Whitfield (1822–71) was a celebrated
African American poet and leader. He was the friend of Frederick
Douglass and Martin R. Delany, and his poetry appeared in a number
of abolitionist and African American journals. In 1853, he published
his first and only volume of poetry, *America and Other Poems*, which
secured his reputation among African American and abolitionist
constituencies. He was profiled as a major African American poet in
Delany's *The Condition, Elevation, Emigration and Destiny of the Colored
People of the United States* (1852), William C. Nell's *The Colored Patriots
of the American Revolution* (1855), and William Wells Brown's *The Black
Man: His Antecedents, His Genius, and His Achievements* (1863). Shortly
after the publication of *America*, Whitfield, who regularly participated
in African American conventions and meetings, emerged as a cham-
pion of the black emigration movement. His pro-emigration letters
appeared in African American newspapers and were republished in
pamphlet form in *Arguments, Pro and Con, on the Call for a National Emi-
gration Convention* (1854). When he moved from his longtime home
in Buffalo, New York, to California in late 1861 or early 1862, he was
embraced by African Americans there as a black nationalist bard. He
became the grand master of the Prince Hall Masons of California and
was viewed by most African Americans in the Northwest as *the* great
African American poet. Among Whitfield's important writings of
the 1860s was a commemorative poem on Lincoln and his accom-
plishments, which he read before thousands at a public occasion in
San Francisco. An anonymous couplet published in the 1867 black

San Francisco newspaper *Pacific Appeal* nicely captures the high esteem, even awe, with which Whitfield was regarded by his contemporaries in California: "Whitfield commands; your aid, O Muses bring! / What muse for Whitfield can refuse to sing."[1]

Hailed as a poetic genius in California, Whitfield achieved little commercial success in his lifetime, and by the time of his death in 1871, he had begun to assume a somewhat invisible place within African American literary and cultural history. But he never quite vanished, remaining, like Ralph Ellison's Invisible Man, a defining, if hard to detect, presence. Whitfield's status of being both there and not there was to some extent anticipated (even ensured) by Martin Delany, who surreptitiously incorporated several poems by Whitfield into his novel, *Blake; or, The Huts of America* (1859, 1861–62), putting them into the mouths (and pens) of Delany-like leaders but without attributing their authorship. (Whitfield had dedicated *America* to Delany.) Whitfield is also evoked in a novel by his great-niece Pauline Hopkins, *Contending Forces* (1900), which includes fictionalized biographical profiles and anecdotes featuring Whitfield's father, mother, and sister, Elizabeth, thereby underscoring how Whitfield's reputation continued to live on through the memory of his extended New England family. Still, during the twentieth century, Whitfield received only dutiful brief mentions in histories of African American poetry, with a poem or two (sometimes more) republished in a few anthologies, and he continues to be little read and underappreciated.[2] And yet his 1853 poetic volume, *America*, which engages the very concept of America, anticipates by two years Walt Whitman's own poetic volume of America, *Leaves of Grass*, and is itself one of the most provocative poetic volumes published in the nineteenth century. Whitfield's current obscurity belies his importance to the history of American poetry as well as his centrality to antebellum debates about the future of blacks in the United States and the larger Americas.

This edition seeks to restore Whitfield's place in the canon of nineteenth-century U.S. poetry and, more specifically, African American literature and intellectual history. We include all of Whitfield's extant published works, including the complete *America* and *Arguments*, which have not been republished since their first appearance during the 1850s. We are hopeful that this volume will contribute to the ongoing rethinking of nineteenth-century African American writing, which is far more variegated than the conventional focus on the slave narrative and novel would suggest. By situating Whitfield in relation to key debates in African American culture, the volume underscores the importance of poetry and periodical culture to black writing during the antebellum and Civil War periods. The volume also underscores the importance of the debate on emigration to blacks' conceptions of the U.S. nation and the Americas and thus helps to illuminate the larger diasporic context of nineteenth-century African American literature.

Perhaps the best introduction to Whitfield comes from the lead article in the Book Notices section of the 29 September 1853 issue of the *Pennsylvania Freeman*. In a laudatory review of Whitfield's 1853 *America*, which concludes by publishing excerpts from two of Whitfield's poems, "America" and "To A. H.," the reviewer prints an excerpt from a correspondent's letter on his travels aboard a steamship out of Dunkirk (a town near Buffalo), where he meets a poet-barber. Here is the review in its entirety:

AMERICA, AND OTHER POEMS. By J. M. WHITFIELD —This is the title of a little volume, recently published by James. S. Leavitt, Buffalo. A copy of it has been sent to us, by a gentleman who met with the author, on the steamer Bay State, while traveling from Dunkirk to Detroit. We can introduce the author to our readers in no better way than by giving them an extract from our correspondent's letter. On entering the barber's shop, on the boat, he noticed that the barber was a man of nearly pure African blood, and a person of unassuming and interesting appearance. He says:

"While shaving me, he asked me very modestly, if I would purchase a book of him. I asked him what book it was? He said it was a volume of poems of his own composition; and handed me one of them. I read the preface and some of the poems, and felt a good deal of interest in the man.

"He told me that the only time he had for reading and writing was in the intervals of labor; and as his business required him to be in his shop early and late, it was difficult for him to get an hour at any time, when he was not liable to interruption.

"He said the object of publishing that volume was to try to get means to support him while he should devote more time to the cultivation of his mind, and to writing, than he was able to do now."

The volume is well worth a perusal. Some of the poems contain stirring thoughts finely expressed. The author, evidently, possesses poetic talent, and noble feeling. We wish him most abundant success.[3]

There is much to be learned from this anecdotal account, which underscores the close connections between Whitfield's labors as a barber and his labors as a poet. We see a black poet who basically had no connection to the publishing worlds of Boston, Philadelphia, and New York and who was forced to market his book in the way of a street (or ship) vendor. The specter of the humble poet who has little time to work on his craft but who heroically persists in his efforts with the hope that he can eventually support himself as a writer has a touch of pathos. As admiring as the review is, with its declarations of Whitfield's "poetic talent, and noble feeling," there is nonetheless something condescending about the portrayal of the "unassuming" poet onboard ship who has surprisingly produced a book that is "well worth a perusal." In a broader sense, the review points to the difficulties that Whitfield and other laboring African American writers would experience not only in trying to develop their art between "intervals of labor" but also in securing their reputations as artists.

Whitfield's barbering was the stuff of folk legend and controversy. Although Douglass regularly honored the efforts of blacks who worked as laborers, he nonetheless lamented Whitfield's situation, declaring in an 1850 issue of the *Anti-Slavery Bugle*: "That talents so commanding, gifts so rare, poetic powers so distinguished, should be tied to the handle of a razor and buried in the precincts of a barber's shop . . . is painfully disheartening." Delany more judgmentally wrote in his 1852 *Condition* that Whitfield's decision to work in the "humble position" of barber is "somewhat reprehensible," asserting that if Whitfield were to "place himself in a favorable situation in life," he "would not be second to John Greenleaf Whittier, nor the late Edgar A. Poe." In his 1855 *Colored Patriots*, William C. Nell remarked on Whitfield's barbershop in Buffalo and then praised Whitfield as a poetic "genius" whose works had "much of the finish of experienced authorship" (with the implication that these works would have had *all* of the finish of experienced authorship if Whitfield had not been tied to a barbershop). The black abolitionist Samuel Ward, on the other hand, saw literary quality and labor going hand in hand, proclaiming in an essay published in the 1854 *Frederick Douglass' Paper* that "James M. Whitfield writes poems that have astonished almost everybody that reads them." But even Ward describes the shipboard Whitfield in a manner that betrays his own patronizing view: "I was desirous of seeing him and expected to find him engaged in some literary pursuits. I found him a cook on board a steam boat, and between the hours of cooking dinner he would scratch off poems which had excited such admiration."[4] As much as Ward admired Whitfield, he saw him as different from, and seemingly inferior to, more comfortably situated poets who worked long hours on their craft.

The image of Whitfield as folksy black laborer was in effect canonized by William Wells Brown in his influential 1863 volume, *The Black Man*. His short discussion of Whitfield begins in this way: "There has long resided in Buffalo, New York, a barber, noted for his scholarly attainments and gentlemanly deportment. Men of the most polished refinement visit his saloon, and, while being shaved, take pleasure in conversing with him; and all who know him feel that he was intended by nature for a higher position in life. This is James M. Whitfield. He is a native of Massachusetts, and removed west some years since." Brown goes on to describe Whitfield's poems as "in good taste and excellent language," but it is difficult not to notice the condescending lament for the poet-barber who, by 1863, had vanished from Brown's sight by moving to California. We can discern the impact of Brown's evaluation in most twentieth-century references to Whitfield, starting with the assessment of Vernon Loggins, who wrote the following in his pioneering *The Negro Author: His Development in America to 1900* (1931): "Possibly the only barber in America who has ever published a volume of verse was James M. Whitfield, a Negro born in Massachusetts but resident most of his life in Buffalo, New York."[5]

True, Whitfield was a barber, but he was also an accomplished poet. His labors did not demean him; on the contrary, his successful entrepreneurship gave him the freedom to explore his interests in poetry and in other political and cultural matters as well. Census records reveal that Whitfield was fairly wealthy for a free black of the period. As was the case for a number of antebellum black barbers, his labors gave him a measure of power and flexibility that most free blacks simply did not have, allowing him to work for the betterment of his family and the larger African American community.[6] Moreover, as Ward's and Brown's comments suggest, his barbering in and of itself was a public and social activity that linked him to the black community, whether onboard ship or at the barbershops that he rented and owned in Buffalo and San Francisco. As the critic Lois Brown remarks, Whitfield's "barbershop, like those of his contemporaries in cities such as Boston and Providence, may have been an essential forum for the free exchange of ideas."[7] In Buffalo and San Francisco, certainly, it is clear that Whitfield used his place of work and his identity as a highly respected community leader and successful local entrepreneur to challenge inequitable laws that would curtail the civic freedoms of African Americans. And like other antebellum black barbers, all of whom had white clients, he would have had a firsthand view of whites' insecurities and vulnerabilities, particularly when placing blade to throat for a shave. In short, Whitfield was an influential poet, leader, and political theorist in part because he was a barber.

It is also worth noting that Whitfield was not born in Massachusetts; he was born in New Hampshire. Anyone glancing at biographical accounts of Whitfield in the standard encyclopedias of literary and national biography would find a welter of confusing claims. Some say Whitfield published a volume in the 1840s; others talk of his travels during the late 1850s and early 1860s to Central and South America. Some say he had a daughter; others refer to two or three sons. We have used the occasion of this edition to develop a fuller and more reliable biographical account of Whitfield's life and career based on sources in journals and newspapers, government documents, minutes from black conventions, and Whitfield's own writings. We have also secured census data and other documents that shed light on Whitfield's family history, and we have drawn on the findings of Lois Brown, whose recent biography of Whitfield's great-niece Pauline Hopkins uncovered new facts about Whitfield's family history in New England, and on Joan R. Sherman's pioneering essay of 1972.[8] As is true for a number of nineteenth-century African American writers and activists, much remains obscure about Whitfield's life. Still, we can offer a relatively authoritative biographical sketch with the expectation that more facts will eventually come to light and help fill the gaps.

James Monroe Whitfield was born in Exeter, New Hampshire, on 10 April 1822, the youngest of the three children of the free blacks Joseph Whitfield and Nancy Paul Whitfield, who had moved there in 1799. Whitfield's father had been born into slavery in Virginia in 1762. As a young man he had escaped to Newburyport, Massachusetts, where in 1797 he married Nancy Paul, a sister of the famous black Baptist ministers Thomas Paul and Nathaniel Paul. The Reverend Thomas Paul was a founding member of Boston's Prince Hall Masons who served as its first chaplain; the Reverend Nathaniel Paul became an influential antislavery activist during the 1820s and 1830s. Other members of the Paul family were educators and social reformers. Although personal circumstances would lead Whitfield to leave

New England when he was still a teenager, his interests in Masonry, black uplift, and antislavery probably had important sources in the inspirational work of his distinguished extended family.[9]

Whitfield's older sister, Elizabeth, married in 1825 when he was still a boy, but he evidently had a close relationship with his brother, Joseph Jr., born sometime between 1814 and 1817, for census records show that they traveled together until the early 1860s. Both probably attended a local school in New Hampshire and were no doubt devastated when their father, a noted hunter and gardener, died of an apparent stroke in 1832. The biographical record gets murky here, but the evidence suggests that Whitfield and his older brother, along with some relatives, moved to Buffalo sometime before 1838. (Or perhaps Whitfield and his brother moved to Buffalo because they had relatives there.)[10] By January 1838, Joseph was sufficiently involved with the African American community in Buffalo to be among the signers of "An Appeal to the Citizens of Buffalo," a petition in which "the respectable part of the colored community" demanded more equitable treatment from Buffalo's white citizenry. That same year, Whitfield, at the age of sixteen, attended an African American convention in Cleveland, perhaps with his brother, and was one of the authors of the convention's resolutions attacking the white-led American Colonization Society for seeking to colonize the free blacks to Africa. Newspaper reports show that Whitfield became increasingly active in Buffalo's African American community, attending meetings in 1840 at Buffalo's Methodist Episcopal Church and at the Union Moral and Mental Improvement Society. The 1840 Buffalo census lists the eighteen-year-old "J. M. Whitfield" as the head of a household of four males and two females, all under the age of thirty-six.[11] That he could assume this role in such a large household suggests that he had taken up the trade of barber by the late 1830s. He would work as a barber for the rest of his life.

During the 1840s, Whitfield remained active in the small African American community in Buffalo. Though African Americans constituted only slightly more than 1 percent of Buffalo's population (census records list approximately 700 blacks in 1850), this was a fluid and politically aggressive community that had an increasingly important place on the Underground Railroad because of the city's proximity to Canada. Whitfield joined hundreds of African Americans at the Methodist Episcopal church on 9 January 1841 to petition the state legislature for "the unrestricted use of the elective franchise to all male citizens being 21 years of age, irrespective of color and condition."[12] He participated in a black reading society (see the eulogy to Thomas Harris in Part 2). Sometime during the early to mid-1840s he married a woman from Connecticut named Frances, also born in 1822, with whom he would have three sons: Charles, born in 1846; Walter, born in 1849; and James Jr., born in 1855 in Ohio.[13] Whitfield may have initially met Delany and Douglass in 1848, when both attended the first national convention of the Free-Soil Party in Buffalo. (Whitman also attended that convention.) One year later, Whitfield published "Stanzas on the First of August," the first of several poems that would appear in Douglass's *North Star*. Whitfield had read "Stanzas" at an August First West Indies emancipation celebration in Buffalo that was attended by the black abolitionist leaders Henry Bibb and Henry Highland Garnet. In 1849 or 1850, Whitfield purchased a house on South Division Street in Buffalo, which would serve as the Whitfields' home until they moved to California in the early 1860s.[14]

As a young man, then, Whitfield by 1850 had become a prominent African American leader and poet. At antislavery meetings, he would generally give a speech, read a poem, or serve on a committee. In October 1850 he attended an anti–Fugitive Slave Law protest meeting, served on the business committee, and continued to publish his poems, some of which were inspired by the politics of the time, while others, like "Ode to Music," had nothing to do with politics. Douglass described Whitfield in the 1850 *Anti-Slavery Bugle* as a "sable son of genius," and Delany described Whitfield in his 1852 *Condition* as "one of the purest poets in America."[15] During this time, both of these black leaders were competing for Whitfield's attention.

Previously friends and coeditors of the *North Star*, Douglass and Delany had publicly broken on the matter of black emigration. Douglass was opposed to all emigration efforts, proclaiming that blacks should demand their rights in the United States, while Delany, in the wake of the Fugitive Slave Law, had become increasingly pessimistic about blacks' prospects and called for selective African American emigration to Central and South America. Douglass held a black convention in Rochester, New York, in 1853, and Whitfield served on a key committee.[16] Shortly after the publication of *America* and his participation in Douglass's convention, Whitfield began attacking Douglass (who had been attacking Delany), publishing several polemical pieces in favor of black emigration in Douglass's own newspaper. His exchange on emigrationism with Douglass and then Douglass's associate editor William J. Watkins was published in 1854 as the compellingly dialogical *Arguments, Pro and Con, on the Call for a National Emigration Convention*. That same year, Whitfield attended Delany's black emigration convention in Cleveland and served on a committee arguing for the importance of promoting black literature. (For more on Whitfield and the debate on emigration, see the introduction to Part 2.)

Following the 1854 Cleveland emigration convention, Whitfield attended other meetings and no doubt shared his ideas about emigration with the African American clientele at his barbershop. He continued writing poetry, which Douglass graciously published in his newspaper. Whitfield attended a black emigration convention in 1856, again in Cleveland, where he served as assistant secretary and was named senior editor of a black periodical that he proposed to the group, possibly publishing one issue. Even while establishing his presence on the national scene, he continued his activist work in Buffalo. During the 1850s Whitfield served as a trustee of the black East Presbyterian Church, and in March 1857 he served as secretary at a meeting held in Buffalo's Vine Street Methodist Church to condemn one William Cooper for using the Fugitive Slave Law to betray "into slavery his wife, who has for more than twenty years been legally free." Buffalo city records of 1858 show that Whitfield owned his own barbershop on 30 East Seneca Street.[17] He may have previously owned another shop or opened this particular East Seneca Street shop years earlier, but the documentation no longer survives.

Although Whitfield seemed ever more settled in Buffalo, there are indications that he began to think seriously about emigrating, perhaps because he thought emigration would be the best way to ensure the future prospects of his sons. That said, Whitfield's movements during the late 1850s remain somewhat unclear. What we do know is that he became intrigued by a plan proposed in 1858 by Congressman Francis Blair of Missouri to use U.S. funds to purchase land in Central America for the colonization of African Americans, and he may have become personally involved with the project. In her biographical overview of Whitfield's career, Joan Sherman states that "Whitfield was probably sent as fact-finding commissioner to Central America in 1859." That claim has been echoed by a number of critics, including Lois Brown, who writes that "on the eve of the Civil War, Whitfield was in Central America, surveying lands that might be ideal for African American relocation." But the questions remain: Who sent Whitfield? And did he really go? The historian Robert L. Harris Jr. asserts that Blair had a Central American Land Company, but Blair's biographer William Parrish makes no mention of that. It is far more likely that such a company was formed by J. Dennis Harris and other African Americans at an 1858 convention of the predominately African American Ohio State Anti-Slavery Society. As Floyd J. Miller reports, by 1859 participants in that convention had organized their own Central American Land Company and announced plans to send a black delegation to find land in Central America that could be acquired for African American emigrants.[18] Whitfield may have been involved with this group, but there is no documentation of his possible travels.

According to Sherman, Buffalo city records indicate that Whitfield lived there until 1859. We have recently discovered federal census records showing that in 1860 James and Frances Whitfield and their three sons moved to New Haven, Connecticut.[19] At that time, James Theodore Holly was organizing the New Haven Pioneer Company of Haytian Emigration, so Whitfield (after possibly making a trip to Central

America with Harris or other African Americans associated with the Central American Land Company) may have been considering joining with one of the most prominent supporters of African American emigration to Haiti. Whitfield was friendly with Holly, and we include in this edition a poem that he wrote in 1856 on the death of Holly's two infant daughters. But again there is no evidence that Whitfield or his family actually made a voyage to Haiti. We do know that in late 1861 or early 1862 Whitfield and his family moved to California, which had been admitted as a free state as part of the Compromise of 1850. Whitfield is listed among the California blacks who submitted a petition in January 1862 urging Congress to set aside money, as Blair proposed, to purchase lands in Central and South America for African American emigration. As the signers of the petition put it, they supported a project that would provide blacks with "some country in which their color will not be a badge of degradation." The petition was also signed by "F. Whitfield," who was in all likelihood Whitfield's wife, Frances, and by Joseph Whitfield.[20]

Despite his apparent support for Blair in that petition, Whitfield, like Delany, abandoned his emigrationism shortly after the start of the Civil War. In 1862 he published a letter about the need for black troops in the Union army, which seems consistent with the politics that informed his approximately two decades in Buffalo, where he was critical of white supremacist slave culture but still held out hope for black citizenship and rights in the United States. During his time in California, Whitfield continued to work for black civil rights, publishing letters and poems in San Francisco newspapers on his hopes for black emancipation and black citizenship. As part of his commitment to black uplift, he joined a San Francisco black Masonic lodge and in 1864 was named grand master of the California order of Prince Hall Masons, a post he held until 1869. During the 1860s, Whitfield traveled extensively in the Northwest. The *Pacific Appeal* of 9 May 1863 reported that Whitfield, "of Shasta co., Cal.," was "en route to Oregon," and there are indications that he spent time in Idaho and Nevada as well. The 1870 census for Elko, Nevada, lists Whitfield as a forty-two-year-old black resident, a barber with a dwelling valued at $1,000 and personal property valued at $500. Whitfield may have temporarily moved to the mining town of Elko (probably in 1869) in an effort to earn extra money for his family, either by mining or working for the railroad, but the reasons for his move remain mysterious. It is also mysterious that he lists Texas on the census form as his place of birth, which may have been his way of indicating that he had crossed the Texas borderlands sometime during 1859–61.[21]

Over the course of the 1860s, San Francisco remained Whitfield's home base for literary pursuits and for practicing his trade as a barber. City records indicate residences at 918 and then 1006 Washington Street and a barbershop at 916 Kearney Street (established sometime around 1865), and newspaper records indicate extensive participation in African American gatherings and celebrations. Early in 1870 he returned to San Francisco, and his last published poem appeared in an April 1870 issue of the *San Francisco Elevator: A Weekly Journal of Progress*. He died in San Francisco on 23 April 1871, at the age of forty-nine, probably of heart disease, and was buried in the city's Masonic cemetery.[22] (For more on Whitfield and California, see the introduction to Part 3.)

Whitfield published poetry from the late 1840s to 1870. His great achievement, and one of the main reasons for this edition, is his 1853 volume, *America and Other Poems*. We believe that Whitfield's *America*, like Whitman's 1855 *Leaves of Grass*, is artfully constructed and shaped and merits consideration as a formally integrated volume. Whitfield begins the volume with "America" and has as its penultimate poem "Stanzas for the First of August," thereby conceiving of America diasporically as including the emancipatory history of the West Indies. But it is significant that the volume includes a number of personal poems that have nothing to do with slavery or race. Whitfield writes about black figures and white figures; he addresses contemporary politics and larger historical forces. In its own distinctive manner, the volume is as fascinating as the first edition of *Leaves of Grass*, especially in its conception of America itself as a kind of poem and the poet as a kind of black nationalist bard who engages multiple aspects of America (ranging from black churches in Buffalo to the pleasures of listening to music in nature). Like the various editions of Whitman's epic, *America* needs to be considered as a coherent whole, however contradictory, rather than as a compilation of discretely unrelated poems ready for the anthologist.[23]

When readers opened *America*, they were exposed to the work of a nineteenth-century African American poet who was preoccupied not only with the question of slavery but equally with other more transcendent topics regarding faith, nature, and artistic creation. *America* as a volume illuminates what it meant to be a nineteenth-century African American poet, revealing a writer who draws on the romantic strains of Byron, the self-reliant transcendentalism of Emerson (Whitfield includes a poem titled "Self-Reliance"), and the urgent political necessity of Douglass and Delany. Of the twenty-four poems in *America*, half address topics other than slavery. Whitfield seems to suggest that if slavery and racism did not exist, he would be able more fully to dedicate his energies to the craft of creating poetry for poetry's sake alone. His divided but ultimately expansive sensibility is underscored by the organization of the volume, in which poems are often staged as counterparts. For example, "Lines on the Death of John Quincy Adams" celebrates a white hero in the American revolutionary tradition, and "To Cinque" celebrates an African hero in a black revolutionary tradition that Whitfield implicitly links to the southern Americas. In a different juxtaposition, Whitfield moves abruptly from a poem about love ("Love") to a poem calling for militant resistance to slavery ("How Long"). Even when two poems are not thematically correlated or juxtaposed, they often share formal properties, such as "Ode to the Fourth of July" and "Ode to Music."

Of course the challenge of becoming a great poet in traditional terms was particularly acute for pre–Civil War African Americans, who had little access to formal education. Whitfield himself seems not to have spent many years in school. But education was clearly important to his extended family, and as a young man in Buffalo, he became involved with and soon was a leader of black literary societies and reading groups. As is true for an important literary predecessor, Phillis Wheatley, and for such African American contemporaries as the poets Daniel Alexander Payne and Frances Harper, Whitfield reveals himself in his poetry as in conversation with a wide range of literary sources. He makes numerous references to the Bible, Greco-Roman mythology, and Eastern religions, and in an effort to link himself to English traditions of poetry, he quotes from or alludes to Shakespeare, Milton, Thomas Gray, Walter Scott, and Lord Byron, among others. Hymns, ballads, and odes are recurrent modes in a volume that exhibits a flair for formalist poetics. *America* contains four occasional hymns that are all celebratory in tone, two about holidays and the other two about the establishment of African American churches. Whitfield's use of the ballad stanza in "Christmas Hymn" and "New Year's Hymn" prefigures Harper's wide use of it in her *Poems on Miscellaneous Subjects* (1854). Even the longer hymn poems about the establishment of black churches make use of octaves that are essentially composed of conjoined ballad stanzas. Whereas Harper often creates conventional ballad stanzas of alternating four- and three-stress lines, Whitfield in his four commemorative hymns makes use of long hymnal meter consisting of rhymes in iambic tetrameter. The formal structure of the ballad stanza allowed Whitfield to fashion some of his poems as songs with an anticipated rhythm and cadence suggestive of his desire to engage a wide readership. Beyond the four hymns, Whitfield's two odes — "Ode for the Fourth of July" and "Ode to Music" — are Horatian odes written in rhyming couplets of lines in tetrameter, with "Ode for the Fourth of July" composed in four octaves and "Ode to Music" in eleven sestets.

The critic Keith D. Leonard identifies African American poets who draw on formalist traditions as "fettered geniuses" in order to emphasize how black poets "fettered" by racism seek to "fetter" themselves to poetic traditions as a way of freeing themselves to develop their poetic art. As Leonard nicely puts it, African American formalists combine "the aesthetic power and social validity of traditional formalist artistry with the complexities of African American experience," even as they emulate "bards in their attempts to become great poets in traditional terms."[24] Whitfield as a poetic formalist often highlights musicality, and his numerous references to songs, choruses, lyres, and harps throughout *America* link him to Poe, Longfellow, Whittier, Harper, and Payne, whose title poem in his 1850 volume *The Pleasures and Other Miscellaneous Poems* literally announces itself as offering a song to pleasure. "To S. A. T." is a variation on the ekphratic poem, prompted by the poet's viewing of a picture in an album. Picking up the harp, the speaker imagines hearing the voice of his beloved, as if the image has suddenly come alive. "Ode to Music" has a similarly mystical tone intimating that a return to nature will lead to a spiritual awareness, and that the ability to commune with nature is itself a kind of religious experience. Music thus gains its importance insofar as it allows one to move closer to the divine, a sensation that is compounded when that singing is performed in the shared community of a chorus.

With his interest in the choral, Whitfield was no doubt influenced by the popular antislavery songs and poems of the time, which were often performed before large, enthusiastic groups of abolitionists. Whittier, for example, who as Delany suggests can be thought of in relation to Whitfield, read and then published a poem called "The Freed Islands" (1846), which celebrated the anniversary of the end of British slavery in the West Indies. Whitfield read his own West Indies emancipation poem, "Stanzas for the First of August," at an 1849 antislavery gathering and included it in *America*. A politically audacious poem, it is placed in the volume right after "Ode to Music" and, in its opening stanza, powerfully links revolution to music:

> FROM bright West Indies' sunny seas,
>   Comes, borne upon the balmy breeze,
> The joyous shout, the gladsome tone,
>   Long in those bloody isles unknown;
> Bearing across the heaving wave
> The song of the unfettered slave.

The "song of the unfettered slave" as the song of freedom is one of the informing motifs of the volume.

In addition to those poems that accentuate Whitfield's engagement with music, *America* features a number of poems that explore art and poetry as particular concerns for nineteenth-century African American writers. In "The Misanthropist," the Byronic speaker finds himself so distraught with the violence before him that he threatens to forsake religion and love altogether. And yet, as he asks the reader how poetry can continue to be created under such social conditions, the poem ironically moves into one of its most musical moments, in a series of anaphoras. In this way, Whitfield contrasts the message of his poem with its formal delivery, a contrast that produces a kind of cognitive dissonance. The question in "The Misanthropist" of whether poetry is possible is revisited in "Yes! Strike Again that Sounding String," with the speaker begging the reader to cease offering songs "of joy and gladness" or of "landscapes bright." Instead the speaker wishes to hear about

> the tempest roaring
> Across the angry foaming deep,
> Or torrents from the mountains pouring
> Down precipices dark and steep.

Whereas the speaker of "The Misanthropist" is dismayed by the violence he witnesses, the speaker in "Yes! Strike Again that Sounding String" welcomes it, offering a warning, akin to Harriet Beecher Stowe's reference to the "San Domingo Hour" in *Uncle Tom's Cabin* (1852) or Douglass's to the "slumbering volcano" in "The Heroic Slave" (1853), that the speaker's anger might indeed soon erupt:

> Thy song may then an echo wake,
> Deep in this soul, long crushed and sad,
> The direful impressions shake
> Which threaten now to drive it mad.

There are suggestions throughout *America* that God's anger might erupt as well. Like Frances Harper and other nineteenth-century African American poets, Whitfield makes frequent use of biblical imagery in his poetry. But whereas Harper, for example, draws on biblical typology to compare African Americans to the Israelites seeking the promised land, Whitfield frequently invokes the figure of an outraged God, akin to that of Jonathan Edwards's "Sinners in the Hands of an Angry God" (1741), who may take vengeance on the nation for its evil ways. Traditional Christian iconography, however, is rarely a governing impulse in *America*. Although Whitfield includes two dedicatory hymns for black churches—the Vine Street African Methodist Episcopal Church and the Michigan Street Baptist Church, both located in Buffalo—his verse does not regularly exploit the Bible or Christianity as other African Americans frequently did to critique the institution of chattel slavery or to compare African Americans to the Israelites who would eventually be led out of bondage. For Whitfield, an eclectic blend of Christianity, world mythology, English literature, and revolutionary politics (particularly with sources in the Enlightenment) comes to the fore in his most political poems against slavery and white supremacism.

Such is the case in Whitfield's best-known poem, "America." The poem begins by directly addressing racism in the context of human rights. Blacks in the United States, the poet declares, are

> Stripped of those rights which Nature's God
> Bequeathed to all the human race,
> Bound to a petty tyrant's nod,
> Because he wears a paler face.

There is much in the overall poem in the Jeffersonian revolutionary tradition and much, in the spirit of Douglass's "What to the Slave Is the Fourth of July?" (1852), pointing to the hypocrisies of the Jeffersonian revolutionary tradition. Given the importance of the American Revolution to the poem, the poet asks his readers directly: "Was it for this, that freedom's fires / Were kindled by your patriot sires?" The key point that Whitfield makes through this couplet, in the spirit of Douglass and William C. Nell, is that "your patriot sires" included black patriots who fought for the Revolutionary cause only to have their children end up as slaves or disenfranchised noncitizens. Whitfield is keen, however, to reiterate that the United States is the "native land" of African Americans. At times adopting a tone similar to Douglass's angrily mocking 1852 speech, Whitfield alludes to a familiar song and turns it into a critique of the United States. The poem's opening visceral lines lull the reader with a degree of familiarity and anticipation only to have that familiarity immediately undercut:

> AMERICA, it is to thee,
> Thou boasted land of liberty, —
> It is to thee I raise my song,
> Thou land of blood, and crime, and wrong.

Echoing and ultimately parodying Samuel Francis Smith's popular "My Country, 'Tis of Thee" (1831), Whitfield illuminates the contrast between the America of the free celebrated in the song and the America of slavery at the heart of his poem.

"America" builds a rhythm of outrage and defiance through its iambic tetrameter and alternating use of rhymed couplets and cross rhymes. And yet it is a poem that does not give up on hope, with the bardic poet emerging in gendered terms as a fighter in the tradition of the white and black participants who fought for their freedom in the Revolutionary War. God has a place in the poem, but men are presented as having the more immediate power to make changes in the world. The poem concludes (and thus the volume begins) with a rousing call for freedom:

> But in the sacred name of peace,
>   Of justice, virtue, love and truth,
> We pray, and never mean to cease,
>   Till weak old age and fiery youth
> In freedom's cause their voices raise,

> And burst the bonds of every slave;
> Till, north and south, and east and west,
> The wrongs we bear shall be redressed.

But it was only after the successful outcome of the Civil War that Whitfield could celebrate, in his 1867 poem on the Emancipation Proclamation, the nation's achievement of "Freedom of thought, and of the pen, / Free schools, free speech, free soil, free men."

For Whitfield, as long as slavery existed in the United States, the country could never emerge as the freedom-loving America of "My Country, 'Tis of Thee"; paeans to the nation would be drowned out by lamentations. Perhaps the most powerful poem in *America* with respect to the nation's fall from its Revolutionary ideals is "The Arch Apostate," which transposes the metaphysics of *Paradise Lost* to the U.S. Senate. Rewriting and reimagining sections of Milton's great epic, Whitfield casts the once exemplary Massachusetts senator Daniel Webster as a Satanic figure who, tempted by desires for national acclaim, chose to vote in favor of the Compromise of 1850, which further extended the domain of slavery and added a strengthened Fugitive Slave Law. Central to the power of the poem is the skillful appropriation of Miltonic imagery and the suspense of not identifying the "apostate" as the celebrated Webster himself until the penultimate line. Just as Satan fell to temptation, Whitfield writes, "So in our Nation's Senate Hall," a statesman, "By far the mightiest of them all, / One called the Godlike," was tempted by "the essence of iniquity" to join "the fiends of hell." Given the despair at the human failings depicted in the poem, it is not surprising that the poem is immediately followed by "The Misanthropist," where the poet as Byronic brooder reflects on how difficult it is to love mankind. And yet that poem is immediately followed by "A Hymn, Written for the Dedication of the Vine Street Methodist Episcopal Church, Buffalo," which presents at least one community where the poet feels at home.

The volume concludes with "The North Star," a poem that Whitfield initially wrote for Douglass's *North Star* but that Whitfield now states in an added footnote happens to be the name of "a newspaper edited by a fugitive slave." Whitfield's use of tempered irony to diminish Douglass's editorial and political stature through a footnote that presents him as the figure of an anonymous fugitive slave (when in fact his freedom had been purchased in 1847) begs the question of *America*'s relation to the debate on black emigration that had come to a head at the time that Whitfield published his volume. Joan Sherman argues that Whitfield's emigrationism centrally informs *America*,[25] but the relationship between politics and poetry in Whitfield's career is much more complicated than such a political interpretation of the volume would suggest. Whitfield in his few extant statements on the matter strongly resisted the notion that black writing must always be about politics, proclaiming in his 1856 "Prospectus of the Afric-American Quarterly Repository," for example, that blacks should write "on all the various branches of literature, art, science, mechanics, law, commerce, philosophy, theology, etc." Moreover, as is true for both Douglass and Delany, Whitfield's politics were constantly in formation and transition. The fact is that most of the poems in *America* were published before Whitfield publicly affiliated himself with Delany's emigrationism, and a number were published in Douglass's newspapers. Though there were considerable differences between Whitfield and his fellow emigrationists, on one hand, and Douglass and his fellow anti-emigrationists, on the other, especially in the years 1853 and 1854, there remained a shared commitment to doing whatever was possible to improve the situation of blacks in the United States, especially given that emigrationism was generally regarded as a selective and not a wholesale solution to the problems facing most African Americans. In short, it would be reductive to term the black nationalism that has an important place in *America* and Whitfield's other political and poetical writings of the period as simply emigrationist or separatist. It would be more accurate to say that *America* and other of Whitfield's writings participated in and helped to shape the debates on black nationalism and emigrationism that were so crucial to the culture of free blacks during the 1850s.

All of Whitfield's writings were engaged with the complicated political scene of the 1850s, and it could be argued that *America*, which had important political sources in what would appear to have been his initial alliance with Douglass, had a role in helping Whitfield to see beyond the U.S. commitments of Douglass. Still, there was much on Whitfield's mind other than politics. He was clearly a deep reader of Shakespeare, Milton, and Byron, and there is every indication in the extant poems published after *America* that Whitfield regarded poetry as a form both of political expression, as in the apocalyptic "The Vision," and of personal or apolitical lyrical expression, as in "Morning Song." Whitfield remained committed to thinking about his poems, whether explicitly political or more personal and lyrical, in relation to literary traditions. In his epic "The Vision," for instance, we see him wrestling with the dystopic tropes of such romantic poems as Byron's "A Dream." A similar sense of poetry as offering opportunities for both political and personal expression, as inflected by various literary traditions, can also be discerned in the poems Whitfield published during his years in California.

With the notable exception of "The Vision," which appeared in three or more installments over the summer of 1853 in *Frederick Douglass' Paper*, and a few short poems, Whitfield did not return to publishing poetry until after he had moved to California in the early 1860s. If the verse in *America* intimates an ambivalence or gloom about the place of blacks in U.S. society because of slavery, then the later poetry of the 1860s signals an increasing belief that freedom and liberty had finally been achieved in the post–Civil War nation. Whitfield's 1867 poem celebrating the fourth anniversary of Abraham Lincoln's Emancipation Proclamation heralds the arrival of a democratic America whose existence had been too long delayed because of the institution of slavery. The poem opens with Whitfield depicting two ships that represent competing cultures that will come into conflict in the future United States. One ship is headed for the Massachusetts Bay Colony and carries freedom-loving Pilgrims; the other heads for Virginia and carries masters and slaves. As the poem develops, Whitfield suggests that those who introduced slavery into North America fashioned an aristocracy in conflict with the democracy established by the Pilgrims. Eradicating slavery, then, is about the need to free the United States from the control of a relatively small number of aristocrats. Deriding U.S. slavery as a cruel aristocracy, he also globalizes the Civil War by enumerating the European soldiers who fought on behalf of the Union as republican warriors. By cataloging these soldiers—including Franz Sigel and Carl Schurz from Germany as well as Thomas Francis Meagher and Michael Corcoran from Ireland—Whitfield links the American Civil War with other freedom movements, suggesting that the world has entered a glorious new era. If his poem celebrating the Emancipation Proclamation internationalizes the Civil War as part of a wider global shift toward liberation, then his last poem, published in 1870, depicts the Civil War as the continuation of the historical progress toward freedom begun by the Greeks and Romans.

Although Whitfield never published another volume after *America and Other Poems*, he remained as active in northern California's black community as he had been more than a decade earlier in Buffalo, with poetry continuing to have a central place in his social and political activities. His 1867 Emancipation Proclamation poem was accompanied by an oration by Ezra R. Johnson, both of which were performed at Platt's Hall on New Year's Day. The poem itself was dedicated to Philip Alexander Bell, editor of the *Elevator*, one of San Francisco's two prominent black periodicals. Bell was an influential African American journalist of the nineteenth century, having started New York's *Weekly Advocate* in 1837. Whitfield's 1868 poem on West Indian emancipation, which again celebrated a wider global shift toward liberation, was read in San Francisco by William Ector, who was from the Caribbean himself. The tonal shift in Whitfield's later poetry toward a greater optimism is due not only to the culmination of the Civil War but also to his love of California. While not devoid of racism, California was as far west as one could get in the continental United States and prob-

ably represented to Whitfield and other African Americans a chance
to start anew, or perhaps it symbolized what a more diverse and free
America might yet become.

Whitfield's life coincided with some of the most important mo-
ments in U.S. history, and his activism and writings were significant
contributions to nineteenth-century African American thought and
culture. His poetry expresses the wide range of sentiment that char-
acterized the sensibilities of many African Americans of his day, with
viewpoints that oscillated between the national and the diasporic in
perspective. Whitfield's capacious writings helped to shape a crucial
moment in the history of nineteenth-century black America; they
can also help to illuminate our understanding of African American
art and politics at the present moment. At the very least, we hope that
our volume will restore Whitfield to a more central place in the on-
going project of recovering and engaging African American literary
and cultural traditions.

NOTES

1. The couplet was part of the unpaginated frontispiece of *Emancipation Oration, by
Dr. Ezra R. Johnson, and Poem, by James M. Whitfield, Delivered at Platt's Hall, January 1,
1867, in Honor of the Fourth Anniversary of President Lincoln's Proclamation of Emancipation*
(San Francisco: Elevator Office, 1867), which reprinted glowing press reviews of the
oration and poem.

2. Delany used three Whitfield poems in his novel; see footnotes 23, 49, and 57 to
America and Other Poems. On Hopkins and Whitfield, see Lois Brown, *Pauline Elizabeth
Hopkins: Black Daughter of the Revolution* (Chapel Hill: University of North Carolina
Press, 2008), esp. 226–27 and 248–49.

3. Book Notices, *Pennsylvania Freeman*, 29 September 1853, 2.

4. Douglass, *Anti-Slavery Bugle*, 24 August 1850, 1; Martin Robison Delany, *The
Condition, Elevation, Emigration and Destiny of the Colored People of the United States*
(Philadelphia: published by the author, 1852), 132; William C. Nell, *The Colored Patriots
of the American Revolution, with Sketches of Several Distinguished Colored Persons: To Which
Is Added a Brief Survey of the Condition and Prospects of Colored Americans* (Boston: Robert
F. Wallcut, 1855), 156; Samuel Ward, "Origin, History and Hopes of the Negro Race,"
Frederick Douglass' Paper, 27 January 1854, 1.

5. William Wells Brown, *The Black Man: His Antecedents, His Genius, and His
Achievements* (Boston: James Redpath, Publisher, 1863), 152, 153; Vernon Loggins, *The

Negro Author: His Development in America to 1900 (New York: Columbia University Press, 1931; Port Washington, N.Y.: Kennikat Press, 1964), 241.

6. In the federal census for 1860, for example, Whitfield, who lists himself as age thirty-eight and by profession a barber, claims $2,000 in real estate holdings, making him among the wealthiest free blacks in his ward (United States Federal Census 1860, Connecticut, New Haven County, New Haven, Connecticut, 6th Ward, visitation 295, 23rd June, James M. Whitfield Family).

7. Brown, *Pauline Elizabeth Hopkins*, 248. See also Douglas Bristol Jr., *Knights of the Razor: Black Barbers in Slavery and Freedom* (Baltimore: Johns Hopkins University Press, 2009), and Xiomara Santamarina, *Belabored Professions: Narratives of African American Working Womanhood* (Chapel Hill: University of North Carolina Press, 2005), which discusses connections between hairdressing and writing in the chapter on Eliza Potter (103–38).

8. See Joan R. Sherman, "James Monroe Whitfield, Poet and Emigrationist: A Voice of Protest and Despair," *Journal of Negro History* 57 (1972): 169–76, and Sherman's chapter on Whitfield in her *Invisible Poets: Afro-Americans of the Nineteenth Century* (Urbana: University of Illinois Press, 1989), 42–52.

9. The Paul family in particular was very distinguished. Whitfield's maternal uncles were renowned ministers, and his cousin Thomas Paul Jr. became the first African American graduate of Dartmouth College. But there is a risk in overstating the influence of the Pauls on Whitfield, who left New England when he was young and subsequently aligned himself with talented black leaders in Buffalo and California. Lois Brown shows in great detail in her excellent *Pauline Elizabeth Hopkins* that Hopkins was obsessed with her family connection to the Pauls and Whitfields, but in Whitfield's own writings from the 1840s to the year of his death, we found not a single reference to the Pauls.

10. The material on Whitfield's parents and childhood draws on Brown, *Pauline Elizabeth Hopkins*, 18, 127, 227. Census records show that the Whitfield brothers lived in Buffalo's Ward 2 for approximately twenty years. The African American George S. Whitfield family lived in Buffalo's nearby Ward 4. Perhaps Whitfield and his brother moved to Buffalo to be with this particular branch of the Whitfield family, or perhaps George moved with Joseph and James from New Hampshire. In census records from 1840 to 1870, James consistently gives his age in accord with an 1822 birthdate, but Joseph gives an 1817 birthdate for the 1850 census, 1814 for the 1855, and 1815 for the 1860 (or else the census recorders made errors). On Joseph, see the United States Federal Census, 1850, 1855, and 1860, all of New York State, Erie County, Buffalo, New York, 2nd Ward.

11. "An Appeal to the Citizens of Buffalo," *Colored American*, 27 January 1838, 1; "Resolutions of the People of Cleveland, on the Subject of African Colonization," *Colored American*, 2 March 1839, 1 (the meeting was held on 12 December 1838); *Colored American*, 4 July 1840, 1; "For the Colored American," *Colored American*, 29 August 1840, 1. On Whitfield's household in 1840, see the United States Federal Census,

1840, New York State, Erie County, Buffalo, New York, 1st Ward, the J. M. Whitfield family.

12. "Great Meeting in Buffalo," *Colored American*, 9 January 1841, 1. On African Americans in Buffalo, see Mark Goldman, *High Hopes: The Rise and Decline of Buffalo, New York* (Albany: State University of New York Press, 1983), chap. 3.

13. In the federal census of 1860, the James. M. Whitfield family provides clear and detailed information: James gives his birthdate as 1822, his place of birth as New Hampshire, and his occupation as barber. His wife, Frances, gives her birthdate as 1822 and her birthplace as Connecticut. James and Frances list three children: Charles, born in 1846 in New York; Walter, born in 1849 in New York; and James Jr., born in 1855 in Ohio (Whitfield had attended an emigration convention in Ohio in 1854, and perhaps this birth occurred shortly after the convention; James's age is listed as six, suggesting an early 1855 birth). See the United States Federal Census, 1860, Connecticut, New Haven County, New Haven, Connecticut, 6th Ward.

14. See "First of August Celebration in Buffalo," *North Star*, 10 August 1849 (which prints Whitfield's poem as part of the article), and Sherman, "James Monroe Whitfield," 173.

15. "Mass Meeting of the Colored Citizens of Buffalo," *North Star*, 24 October 1850, 1; Douglass, "Our Western Anti-Slavery Tour," *Anti-Slavery Bugle*, 24 August 1850, 1; Delany, *Condition*, 132.

16. Whitfield attended Douglass's convention a year after serving on a special committee of Buffalo's African Americans urging him to hold his convention in Buffalo. See *Frederick Douglass' Paper*, 3 September 1852, which reports on a meeting at Buffalo's Michigan Street Baptist Church, where a committee of five, including Whitfield, offered the following resolution: "Whereas, we have learned that a Colored National Convention is about to be held at some point in the United States not already specified; and, whereas, we believe Buffalo to be the most central place for holding such Convention; therefore, Resolved, That we do most cordially invite the Convention to hold its session in this city" (1).

17. *Buffalo Courier*, 5 March 1857, 1. See also "Abstract of the Minutes of the Cleveland National Convention," *Provincial Freeman*, 25 November 1856, 1; Monroe Fordham, *A History of Bethel A.M.E. Church, Buffalo, New York, 1831–1977* (Buffalo: Bethel History Society, 1978), 9; and Sherman, "James Monroe Whitfield," 173.

18. Sherman, "James Monroe Whitfield," 175; Brown, *Pauline Elizabeth Hopkins*, 250. See also Robert L. Harris Jr., "H. Ford Douglass: Afro-American Antislavery Emigrationist," *Journal of Negro History* 62 (1977): 217–34; William E. Parrish, *Frank Blair: Lincoln's Conservative* (Columbia: University of Missouri Press, 1998); J. Dennis Harris, *A Summer on the Borders of the Caribbean Sea* (1860), in *Black Separatism and the Caribbean, 1860*, ed. Howard H. Bell (Ann Arbor: University of Michigan Press, 1970); and Floyd J. Miller, *The Search for a Black Nationality: Black Emigration and Colonization, 1787–1863* (Urbana: University of Illinois Press, 1975), 237–38. For more on Blair, see Whitfield's letter to Blair in Part 2.

19. See n. 12.

20. See *Memorial of Leonard Dugged, George A. Bailey, and other free colored persons of California, praying Congress to provide means for their colonization to some country in which their color will not be a badge of degradation* (Washington, D.C.: House of Representatives, 37th Congress, 2d session, Misc. Doc., No., 31, 1862).

21. *Pacific Appeal*, 9 May 1863, 2. In the 1870 census, Whitfield is listed as living with two other African American men. See the United States Federal Census, Nevada, Elko County, Elko, Nevada, 2nd Ward, dwelling 49, 3rd June. At some point during the 1860s, Joseph Whitfield returned to Buffalo, where he died in 1870.

22. See Sherman, "James Monroe Whitfield," 175–76. Sherman notes that the death certificate gives Whitfield's residence as 111 Prospect Street in San Francisco. On Whitfield and Freemasonry, see William H. Grimshawe, *Official History of Freedom Masonry among the Colored People of North America* (1903; New York: Negro Universities Press, 1969), 218.

23. The best discussion of *America* as a simultaneously coherent and contradictory volume is Edward Whitley's "James M. Whitfield: The Poet of Slaves," chapter 1 of his *American Bards: Walt Whitman and Other Unlikely Candidates for National Poet* (Chapel Hill: University of North Carolina Press, 2010). Three poems from *America* are reprinted in Joan R. Sherman's *African-American Poetry of the Nineteenth Century: An Anthology* (Urbana: University of Illinois Press, 1992), and three appear in *The Norton Anthology of African American Literature* (2nd ed., 2003). Readers need to be able to take the full measure of *America* as a volume. For useful discussions of the poetic volume qua volume, see *Poems in Their Place: The Intertextuality and Order of Poetic Collections*, ed. Neil Fraistat (Chapel Hill: University of North Carolina Press, 1986).

24. Keith D. Leonard, *Fettered Genius: The African American Bardic Poet from Slavery to Civil Rights* (Charlottesville: University of Virginia Press, 2006), 12.

25. In "James Monroe Whitfield," Sherman underscores the close connections between Whitfield's "two avocations: writing poetry and championing the cause of black separatism" (170).

A Note on the Texts

Most of the poems, essays, and letters in this edition have not been republished since their first appearance in the mid-nineteenth century. Whitfield published his work in African American newspapers, convention proceedings, and other such outlets, and he published his one book of poems with a small press in Buffalo. Additionally, he published his letters on black emigration, some of which had first appeared in *Frederick Douglass' Paper*, in a volume brought out by a small press in Detroit. All of the texts in this edition are drawn from their first printings or their immediate republication in book form. Given that Whitfield was not publishing with large presses, one would expect numerous printers' errors, but the number is surprisingly small. Still, there are errors, which we have chosen silently to correct. We have preserved all nineteenth-century usages and spellings.

PART I *America*

In 1853, the James S. Leavitt Company, a relatively small press in Buffalo known for its Universalist and Unitarian publications,[1] brought out Whitfield's first and only collection, *America and Other Poems*. Dedicated to Martin R. Delany, whose emigrationist politics Whitfield had recently embraced, the volume consisted of twenty-four poems, at least eight of which had been previously published in Frederick Douglass's newspapers. Other poems may have appeared in more obscure African American newspapers. The book measured approximately four by six inches and was bound with soft covers in the manner of a pamphlet. The small size and light weight would have facilitated the efforts of Whitfield, and perhaps others, to peddle a dozen or so books at a time. Whitfield sold copies of the book at his barbershop and onboard ships, where he sometimes worked as a barber. Easily rolled up or folded, *America* could be carried in one's shirt or pants pocket and passed from one reader to another.[2]

Whitfield's contractual relationship with the Leavitt Company is unclear. There was broad sympathy for abolitionism among Universalists, Unitarians, and other liberal Protestant groups in the Northeast, so Leavitt may have offered a royalties contract for a volume by the city's leading black poet. Or, just as likely, Whitfield may have used some of his savings from barbering to commission Leavitt as his publisher and then actively vended copies in order to recover his initial investment. We get some sense of Whitfield's situation from *America*'s anonymous introduction, which reports that Whitfield works as a barber and "writes in such intervals of leisure as he is able to realize." The author of the introduction self-identifies with Whitfield as an African American and hopes that the volume will succeed with "our people." In all likelihood, the author of the introduction is Whitfield himself. After all, who else would have known that Whitfield "feels the 'Divine spark' within"? Like William Wells Brown, who anonymously introduced his novel *Clotel*, published the same year as *America*, Whitfield may have wanted to avoid the typical situation of having a white editor introduce (and in some ways appropriate) a black text.[3] The self-authored introduction triumphantly announces the advent of a black American poet who has composed, organized, and published a volume of poetry on his own terms.

Despite the relative obscurity of the press, *America* received considerable attention, garnering reviews in the most prominent antislavery newspapers of the time: William Lloyd Garrison's *Liberator*, Douglass's *Frederick Douglass' Paper*, and Mary Ann Shadd's *Provincial Freeman*, which was the most influential black journal in Canada. As noted in our introduction, *America* was also reviewed in the *Pennsylvania Freeman*, and it was probably reviewed in other small-circulation black abolitionist newspapers as well. Reviewers hailed the volume. Douglass's regular reviewer and business manager, Julia Griffiths, declared in *Frederick Douglass' Paper* that "Mr. Whitfield is a genius, and a genuine lover of the muses." Garrison asserted in the *Liberator* that Whitfield "evinces genius of no common order." The anonymous reviewer in the *Provincial Freeman* exclaimed that Whitfield is "entitled to a first place among the colored men, known as such in the United States, who have been inspired by the Muses," concluding that a copy of *America* "should be in every family."[4] In addition to praising Whitfield's poetic genius, reviewers typically offered a sampling from the book and in this way helped to circulate Whitfield's poems to those who might not have access to a bookseller with the volume.[5] Douglass and Griffiths also reprinted one of Whitfield's poems in their fundraising collection, *Autographs for Freedom* (1853), thereby linking Whitfield with such popular writers as Harriet Beecher Stowe, Catharine Sedgwick, and John Greenleaf Whittier, who were also contributors.[6]

America secured Whitfield's contemporary reputation as a great African American poet, but that reputation could not make a career. Despite his entrepreneurial efforts at selling his well-received book in Buffalo and elsewhere, the volume failed to provide him with the income he needed to become a full-time author, and his poetry writing became more sporadic. Over the next eighteen years, Whitfield would nevertheless strive "to cultivate, improve, and fully develop the talent which God hath given him" (as he puts it in the introduction to *America*), and poetry would remain central to his work as an antislavery activist and reformer—and to his sense of himself as an artist. We are pleased to make available to a new generation of readers the complete text of Whitfield's elegant, intense, and wide-ranging *America*, a poetic volume that addresses America through the eyes of a poet whose imagination remained unconstrained by the nation.

NOTES

1. Stephen Rensselaer's *Historical Sketches and Incidents Illustrative of the Establishment and Progress of Universalism in the State of New York* (1848) is a typical Leavitt publication; the Leavitt company also published Universalist sermons, church histories, and (beginning in the 1850s) the annual reports of the Buffalo Young Men's Christian Association. Whatever the contractual situation, *America* may have been hastily produced, because there are some obvious errors. For instance, the contents page is missing one poem, "The North Star," and lists the title of "Stanzas for the First of August" (which is correctly titled near the close of the volume) as "Stanzas for the month of August."

2. There is evidence that the volume had a significant life in the culture after its publication in 1853, passed from reader to reader and sometimes even rebound in more sturdy and attractive covers and presented as gifts. The American Antiquarian Society, for example, holds a volume that was rebound in cloth and stamped with leaves on the front and back covers. This particular volume was given as a gift in 1859 by one W. I. Currier, whose nameplate is glued onto the inside front cover, to George W. Sleeper. (Our thanks to Ezra Greenspan for sharing this information; Greenspan speculates that the book was a gift from a teacher to a student.) Unlike this attractively bound volume, most copies of *America*, as they circulated from reader to reader and from household to household, fell apart over the years or were lost. The tattered copy from the Library of Congress that we initially consulted in 2001 for this edition is now missing, and WorldCat lists fewer than thirty extant volumes.

3. See John Sekora's classic "Black Message / White Envelope: Genre, Authenticity, and Authorship in the Antebellum Slave Narrative," *Callaloo* 32 (1987): 482–515,

and Robert Stepto, *From behind the Veil: A Study of Afro-American Narrative* (Urbana: University of Illinois Press, 1979), 6–7. For another notable black self-introduction from the period, see Harriet E. Wilson's *Our Nig; or, Sketches from the Life of a Free Black* (1859).

4. *Frederick Douglass' Paper*, 15 July 1853, 3 (the review is signed J. G., for Julia Griffiths); *Liberator*, 18 November 1853, 3 (the review is signed ED. LIB., for Garrison, the editor of the *Liberator*); *Provincial Freeman*, 15 July 1854, 3.

5. For instance, accompanying the review in the 18 November 1853 issue of the *Liberator* were three poems from *America*: "Self-Reliance," "Delusive Hope," and "Ode for the Fourth of July."

6. Douglass and Griffiths reprinted Whitfield's "How Long?" See *Autographs for Freedom* (Boston: J. P. Jewett, 1853), 46–54.

AMERICA

AND OTHER

POEMS

BY J. M. WHITFIELD

BUFFALO
PUBLISHED BY JAMES S. LEAVITT

1853

TO

MARTIN R. DELANY, M.D.[1]

THIS VOLUME

IS INSCRIBED AS A SMALL TRIBUTE OF RESPECT

FOR HIS CHARACTER,

ADMIRATION OF HIS TALENTS, AND LOVE OF HIS PRINCIPLES,

BY THE

AUTHOR.

1. Martin R. Delany (1812–85) apprenticed as a doctor in Pittsburgh during the 1830s and 1840s and attended Harvard Medical School for one semester in the fall of 1850, before he was dismissed at the request of the white students. He continued to practice medicine during the 1850s, a time when he broke with Frederick Douglass and emerged as one of the leading black emigrationists and writers of the period. Among his major works are *The Condition, Elevation, Emigration and Destiny of the Colored People of the United States* (1852), "Political Destiny of the Colored Race on the American Continent" (1854), and the novel *Blake* (1859–62).

CONTENTS

INTRODUCTION

"ANOTHER book of poetry," exclaims the reader; "and that, too, by one of the proscribed race, whose lot has been ignorance and servitude." It is even so: and this little volume is presented to the public in the full confidence that it will be read and appreciated, when the circumstances of its origin are known. Its merits as a literary production, we leave to be decided upon by the kind judgment of the American people. We do not claim that the poetry is of the highest order: but we do claim that it would be creditable to authors of greater pretensions than the humble colored man, who hath wrought it out amid the daily and incessant toil necessary for the maintenance of a family, who are dependent upon the labor of his hands for support. There is in it the fire of a genius which, under more favored circumstances, would have soared high, and obtained no mean place in the world's estimation. There is the voice of true poesy speaking in it, which, though in the rough it may be, and wanting the polish which education and refined opportunity give, yet nature outgusheth in harmonious numbers, and her bard, all untutored as he is, singeth sweetly, and giveth forth the conceptions of his soul in "words that breathe and thoughts that burn."[2]

The writer of the following pages is a poor colored man of this city, engaged in the humble, yet honorable and useful occupation of a barber. His time is constantly taken up in his business, and he writes in such intervals of leisure as he is able to realize. He is uneducated; not

2. Drawn from the British poet Thomas Gray's "The Progress of Poesy" (1757), line 110.

entirely, but substantially; his genius is native and uncultivated, and yet his verse possesses much of the finish of experienced authorship; there is the "ring of the true metal" in it. He feels the "Divine spark" within him, and longs for the means and opportunity to call in the aid of intellectual culture, that he may be enabled to give it form and shape, and clothe it in befitting language. This volume is presented to the public with this view, and in the hope that it may find a favorable reception with our people, and "put money in the purse"[3] of the writer, that he may be able to cultivate, improve, and fully develop the talent which God hath given him.

BUFFALO, MAY, 1853

---

3. Paraphrase of Iago's instructions to Roderigo in Shakespeare's *Othello* (act 1, scene 3).

POEMS

AMERICA

AMERICA, it is to thee,
Thou boasted land of liberty,—
It is to thee I raise my song,
Thou land of blood, and crime, and wrong.[4]
It is to thee, my native land,
From whence has issued many a band
To tear the black man from his soil,
And force him here to delve and toil;
Chained on your blood-bemoistened sod,
Cringing beneath a tyrant's rod,
Stripped of those rights which Nature's God
   Bequeathed to all the human race,
Bound to a petty tyrant's nod,
   Because he wears a paler face.
Was it for this, that freedom's fires
Were kindled by your patriot sires?
Was it for this, they shed their blood,
On hill and plain, on field and flood?
Was it for this, that wealth and life

---

4. The opening lines rewrite through parody Samuel Francis Smith's popular patriotic song "America" (1831), which begins, "My country, 'tis of thee, / Sweet land of liberty, / Of thee I sing." On traditions in antislavery poetry of responding to Smith's song, see Robert James Branham, "'Of Thee I Sing': Contesting 'America,'" *American Quarterly* 48 (1996): 623–50.

Were staked upon that desperate strife,
Which drenched this land for seven long years
With blood of men, and women's tears?
When black and white fought side by side,[5]
    Upon the well-contested field,—
Turned back the fierce opposing tide,
    And made the proud invader yield—
When, wounded, side by side they lay,
    And heard with joy the proud hurrah
From their victorious comrades say
    That they had waged successful war,
The thought ne'er entered in their brains
That they endured those toils and pains,
To forge fresh fetters, heavier chains
For their own children, in whose veins
Should flow that patriotic blood,
So freely shed on field and flood.
Oh no; they fought, as they believed,
    For the inherent rights of man;
But mark, how they have been deceived
    By slavery's accursed plan.
They never thought, when thus they shed
    Their heart's best blood, in freedom's cause,
That their own sons would live in dread,
    Under unjust, oppressive laws:
That those who quietly enjoyed
    The rights for which they fought and fell,
Could be the framers of a code,
    That would disgrace the fiends of hell!

---

5. Black abolitionists had long argued that African Americans had a key role in the American Revolutionary War and that blacks therefore had earned their freedom through blood. That argument was given new force by the Boston-based black abolitionist William C. Nell, who in 1851 published *Services of Colored Americans, in the Wars of 1776 and 1812*, which he would expand into *The Colored Patriots of the American Revolution* (1855).

Could they have looked, with prophet's ken,
    Down to the present evil time,
    Seen free-born men, uncharged with crime,
Consigned unto a slaver's pen,—
Or thrust into a prison cell,
With thieves and murderers to dwell—
While that same flag whose stripes and stars
Had been their guide through freedom's wars
As proudly waved above the pen
Of dealers in the souls of men!
Or could the shades of all the dead,
    Who fell beneath that starry flag,
Visit the scenes where they once bled,
    On hill and plain, on vale and crag,
By peaceful brook, or ocean's strand,
    By inland lake, or dark green wood,
Where'er the soil of this wide land
    Was moistened by their patriot blood,—
And then survey the country o'er,
    From north to south, from east to west,
And hear the agonizing cry
Ascending up to God on high,
From western wilds to ocean's shore,
    The fervent prayer of the oppressed;
The cry of helpless infancy
    Torn from the parent's fond caress
By some base tool of tyranny,
    And doomed to woe and wretchedness;
The indignant wail of fiery youth,
    Its noble aspirations crushed,
Its generous zeal, its love of truth,
    Trampled by tyrants in the dust;
The aerial piles which fancy reared,
    And hopes too bright to be enjoyed,

Have passed and left his young heart seared,
   And all its dreams of bliss destroyed.
The shriek of virgin purity,
   Doomed to some libertine's embrace,
Should rouse the strongest sympathy
   Of each one of the human race;
And weak old age, oppressed with care,
   As he reviews the scene of strife,
Puts up to God a fervent prayer,
   To close his dark and troubled life.
The cry of fathers, mothers, wives,
   Severed from all their hearts hold dear,
And doomed to spend their wretched lives
   In gloom, and doubt, and hate, and fear;
And manhood, too, with soul of fire,
And arm of strength, and smothered ire,
Stands pondering with brow of gloom,
Upon his dark unhappy doom,
Whether to plunge in battle's strife,
And buy his freedom with his life,
And with stout heart and weapon strong,
Pay back the tyrant wrong for wrong,
Or wait the promised time of God,
   When his Almighty ire shall wake,
And smite the oppressor in his wrath,
And hurl red ruin in his path,
And with the terrors of his rod,
   Cause adamantine hearts to quake.
Here Christian writhes in bondage still,
   Beneath his brother Christian's rod,
And pastors trample down at will,
   The image of the living God.
While prayers go up in lofty strains,
   And pealing hymns ascend to heaven,

The captive, toiling in his chains,
    With tortured limbs and bosom riven,
Raises his fettered hand on high,
    And in the accents of despair,
To him who rules both earth and sky,
    Puts up a sad, a fervent prayer,
To free him from the awful blast
    Of slavery's bitter galling shame—
Although his portion should be cast
    With demons in eternal flame!
Almighty God! 't is this they call
    The land of liberty and law;
Part of its sons in baser thrall
    Than Babylon or Egypt saw—
Worse scenes of rapine, lust and shame,
    Than Babylonian ever knew,
Are perpetrated in the name
    Of God, the holy, just, and true;
And darker doom than Egypt felt,[6]
May yet repay this nation's guilt.
Almighty God! thy aid impart,
And fire anew each faltering heart,
And strengthen every patriot's hand,
Who aims to save our native land.
We do not come before thy throne,
    With carnal weapons drenched in gore,
Although our blood has freely flown,
    In adding to the tyrant's store.
Father! before thy throne we come,
    Not in the panoply of war,

---

6. See Exodus 7–12, which describes the plagues inflicted on the Egyptians for enslaving the Israelites.

With pealing trump, and rolling drum,
   And cannon booming loud and far;
Striving in blood to wash out blood,
   Through wrong to seek redress for wrong;
For while thou 'rt holy, just and good,
   The battle is not to the strong;
But in the sacred name of peace,
   Of justice, virtue, love and truth,
We pray, and never mean to cease,
   Till weak old age and fiery youth
In freedom's cause their voices raise,
And burst the bonds of every slave;
Till, north and south, and east and west,
The wrongs we bear shall be redressed.

CHRISTMAS HYMN

HAIL, glorious morn! whose radiant beams,
   Looked down on Christ's nativity,
For every year thy presence teems
   With joy and glad festivity.

On Judea's plains[7] th' angelic throng
   Burst on the shepherds' awe-struck gaze,
And raised on high a new-made song
   Unto their great Creator's praise.

The star of Bethlehem's heavenly light
   Guided the wise men from the east,
Who came to lay their power and might,
   Their wisdom, at the Saviour's feet.

---

7. Southernmost region of ancient Palestine.

Oh, may that star's resplendent light
   Continue o'er the world to shine,
Till nations now in Pagan night
   Shall worship at thy holy shrine.

Till all the people of the earth,
   From north to south, from east to west,
Hear tidings of the Saviour's birth,
   And bow unto his great behest.

Till superstition's blighting sway
   Shall flee before religion's light,
As doth the glorious orb of day
   Disperse the shadows of the night.

LINES ON THE DEATH OF JOHN QUINCY ADAMS[8]

THE great, the good, the just, the true,
   Has yielded up his latest breath;
The noblest man our country knew,
   Bows to the ghastly monster, Death;
The son of one whose deathless name
   Stands first on history's brightest page;
The highest on the list of fame
   As statesman, patriot, and sage.

---

8. The son of Abigail Adams and John Adams, the second president of the United States, John Quincy Adams (1767–1848) served as the sixth president of the United States (1825–29). Soon after leaving office, he was elected to Congress and became a vociferous opponent of slavery. He took particular aim at the gag rules that prohibited the acknowledgment and consideration of antislavery petitions in Congress. In 1841 Adams participated in the defense of the Amistad slave rebels in a case that the Supreme Court decided in favor of Joseph Cinqué and the other West Africans on the Spanish slaver.

In early youth he learned to prize
    The freedom which his father won;
The mantle of the patriot sire,
    Descended on his mightier son.
Science, her deepest hidden lore
    Beneath his potent touch revealed;
Philosophy's abundant store,
    Alike his mighty mind could wield.

The brilliant page of poetry
    Received additions from his pen,
Of holy truth and purity,
    And thoughts which rouse the souls of men!
Eloquence did his heart inspire,
    And from his lips in glory blazed,
Till nations caught the glowing fire,
    And senates trembled as they praised!

While all the recreant of the land
    To slavery's idol bowed the knee—
A fawning, sycophantic band,
    Fit tools of petty tyranny—
He stood amid the recreant throng,
    The chosen champion of the free,
And battled fearlessly and long
    For justice, right, and liberty.

What though grim Death has sealed his doom
    Who faithful proved to God and us;
And slavery, o'er the patriot's tomb
    Exulting, pours its deadliest curse;
Among the virtuous and free
    His memory will ever live;
Champion of right and liberty,
    The blessings, truth and virtue give.

TO CINQUE[9]

ALL hail! thou truly noble chief,
    Who scorned to live a cowering slave;
Thy name shall stand on history's leaf,
    Amid the mighty and the brave:
Thy name shall shine, a glorious light
    To other brave and fearless men,
Who, like thyself, in freedom's might,
    Shall beard the robber in his den.
Thy name shall stand on history's page,
    And brighter, brighter, brighter glow,
Throughout all time, through every age,
    Till bosoms cease to feel or know
    "Created worth, or human woe."
Thy name shall nerve the patriot's hand
    When, 'mid the battle's deadly strife,
The glittering bayonet and brand
    Are crimsoned with the stream of life:
When the dark clouds of battle roll,
And slaughter reigns without control,
Thy name shall then fresh life impart,
And fire anew each freeman's heart.
Though wealth and power their force combine
    To crush thy noble spirit down,
There is above a power divine
    Shall bear thee up against their frown.[10]

9. Joseph Cinqué (ca. 1813–79) was one of the leaders of the bloody slave revolt aboard the Spanish slaver *Amistad* in 1839. Soon after the mutiny, which occurred off the coast of Cuba, the ship was seized by the U.S. navy and the rebels were imprisoned in New Haven. Influenced by the speeches of John Quincy Adams and others, the U.S. Supreme Court freed the captives in March 1841. Cinqué returned to Sierra Leone in 1842.

10. In a bold act of appropriation and recontextualization, Martin Delany reprints "To Cinque" in chapter 60 of his serialized novel *Blake*, dropping the title and attributing the poem to those who are celebrating the heroic black leadership of Blake and the Cuban poet-rebel Placido.

NEW YEAR'S HYMN

ANOTHER year, another year,
    Unfolds its page of hope and fear!
Where, at its close, shall we appear
    Who now are congregated here.

Perhaps, with those now passed away,
    We may be laid deep in the earth;
Perchance, 'mid foreign scenes, we may
    Forget the land that gave us birth.

Perhaps upon the stormy seas,
    Where raging billows wildly roll,
The terrors of despair may seize
    Upon the dark and guilty soil.

But wheresoe'er our footsteps tend,
    'Mid tropic sands, or polar snow,
May we remember that great Friend
    Who guards us wheresoe'er we go.

Whose mighty hand hath been our stay
    Through scenes of trouble, doubt and fear,
And suffered us, poor worms of clay,
    To enter on another year.

TO A. H.[11]

I JUST had turned the classic page,
    With ancient lore and wisdom fraught,
Which many a hoary-headed sage
    Had stamped with never-dying thought;
And many a bard of lofty mind,
    With measured lay and tuneful lyre,
And strains too grand for human kind,
    All pregnant with celestial fire —
In notes majestic, loud and long,
Had poured the volumed tide of song.
Here Egypt's sages, skilled of yore
    In Isis' dark mysterious rites,[12]
Unvailed their fund of mystic lore
    To eager Grecian neophytes.
And as I sadly musing sat,
    Thinking on ages long gone by,
The Pantheon[13] arose in state,
    And passed before my fancy's eye.
Juno's majestic mien was there,
    And Venus' beauteous form and face,
Diana, modest, chaste, and fair,
    Hebe, adorned with youthful grace,
Ceres, with sheaves and plenteous horn,
    Minerva, with high wisdom crowned,
Aurora, radiant as the morn,
    Whose smiles shed light on all around;

---

11. First published in the *North Star*, 12 April 1850, 4. Despite the use of the abbreviation "A. H.," which remains obscure, this and other of Whitfield's love poems are perhaps best read as verses about love and poetry (*ars poetica*) that do not necessarily need a "real-life" referent.

12. Isis was the Egyptian goddess of the dead, known for reassembling the body of her dead husband, Osiris, so that she could impregnate herself, giving birth to Horus, the first ruler of a united Egypt.

13. The Pantheon was a Roman temple constructed circa 27 B.C.E.

The Graces, sisterhood divine,
　　Prepared to charm each mortal sense,
And last of all, the immortal Nine,[14]
　　With music, verse, and eloquence,—
Naiads and Nymphs,[15] a numerous train,
Came thronging through the ample fane.
Peris, from eastern regions came,
　　Bearing aloft the sacred fire,
Which Zoroaster, son of flame,
　　Kindled on Mithra's ancient pyre.[16]
The dark-eyed maids who wait to greet
　　The Moslem brave in Paradise,
Forsook awhile their blissful seat,
　　And left the region of the skies,
The palm of beauty to dispute
With sovereign Jove's[17] immortal suit.
And as I sat, entranced, amazed,
　　With radiant beauty circled round,
Thy form, high o'er the rest upraised,
　　Appeared, with brighter splendor crowned
And every eye was turned on thee,
　　Of Houri,[18] Peri, Goddess, Grace,

14. Whitfield refers to a number of Greek and Roman gods and goddesses: Juno, queen of the gods and protector of the Roman state; Venus, Roman goddess of love and beauty; Diana, Roman goddess of nature and fertility; Hebe, Greek goddess of youth; Ceres, Roman goddess of agriculture; Minerva, Roman goddess of wisdom; Aurora, Roman personification of the dawn; the Graces, the three Roman goddesses providing talent and inspiration; the immortal Nine, the Greek goddesses (muses) who inspire the arts and sciences.

15. In Greek myth, naiads are beautiful, lighthearted, and beneficent nymphs associated with flowing water (i.e., springs, rivers, fountains, lakes); nymphs are female divinities often associated with fertility and nature.

16. References to Iranian/Zoroastrian mythology. Peris were benevolent, graceful spirits; Zoroaster was the founder and prophet of Zoroastrianism (a dualistic ancient Persian religion); Mithra was the Iranian god of light and friendship.

17. Jove, also known as Jupiter, was the Roman god of light and sky, protector of the state.

18. A houri is a nymph generally linked in Islamic tradition to the heavenly paradise described in the Koran.

As, bright in peerless majesty,
    You mounted to the highest place.
Juno resigned her crown to thee,
    Venus her zone of love unbound,
While haughty Pallas[19] bowed the knee,
    And laid her armor on the ground.
The Muses, also, owned thee queen
    Of music, eloquence, and verse,
And tuned their lyres and harps, I ween,
    Thy matchless praises to rehearse.
The Peri owned thy dazzling eye
    Might kindle far a brighter fire
Than that which erst blazed to the sky,
    On many an oriental pyre,
There lighting up with ray divine,
The ancient Gheber's[20] fiery shrine.
The Houris owned that could thy charms
    Be viewed from regions of the skies,
'T would tempt the faithful from their arms,
    And all the joys of Paradise;
Or were the Prophet's self on earth,
    And but a glimpse of thee were given,
He'd own one smile of thine were worth
    All pleasures of his highest Heaven;
And from the Moslem creed erase
    That portion so unjustly given,
Which shuts one half the human race
    Forever from the joys of Heaven.
And all the bright Olympic train,
Finding the contest waged in vain,
And that each boasted Deity

19. Pallas Athena, Greek goddess of war, wisdom, and justice.
20. Gabar, an Iranian Zoroastrian.

Was far eclipsed in charms by thee,
Fled from the scene where all their charms,
    The power of wisdom, beauty, grace,
Had prostrate sunk beneath the arms
    Of one who, though of mortal race,
In her own person did combine
All of the attributes divine
Which Grecian fancy erst did trace
In Nymph, in Goddess, or in Grace;
And ne'er did eastern poet tell,
'Mid all the fabled sprites that dwell
On earth, in water, or in air,
Of aught that could with thee compare—
Of mortal, or immortal kind,
In grace of person and of mind:
For in thy presence pleasures grow,
    And brightest glories round thee move,
Whether it be with men below,
    Or seraphs in the realms above
And when thy spirit shall return
    Back to that Heaven from whence it came,
Angels and seraphs, in their turn,
    Shall join to celebrate thy name,
And spread through Heaven as well as earth,
The story of thy matchless worth.

LOVE

IN the bright dreams of early youth,
    I strung my lyre, and waked a strain,
In praise of friendship, love and truth,
    Without a thought of care or pain;
    But soon, in answer to my strain,

A voice came pealing from above;
　Sounding o'er valley, hill and plain—
Where's he that knows the power of love?

The brainless youth in lady's bower,
　Who, sighing, chants some amorous lay,
Or twines a wreath, or plucks a flower,
　A tribute of his love to pay
　Or, mid the crowd, the gallant gay,
With witty jest, and jibe, and jeer,
　Spending in revelry and play
The few bright hours allowed him here,

Thinks that he knows what 't is to love—
　Speaks of that pure and holy flame
Which emanates from God above,
　As though 't were nothing but a name
　That noble, pure, and holy flame,
Jehovah's chiefest attribute,
　Implanted in the human frame,
Raised man above the sordid brute.

And he who ever feels its power,
　Whate'er his station, high or low,
In pleasure's or in sorrow's hour,
　Will feel his inmost bosom glow
　With love to all, both friend and foe;
For God commandeth all to love,
　And those who would his glories know,
Must learn this truth, that God is love.[21]

21. See 1 John 4:8.

HOW LONG[22]

HOW long, oh gracious God! how long
    Shall power lord it over right?
The feeble, trampled by the strong,
    Remain in slavery's gloomy night.[23]
In every region of the earth,
    Oppression rules with iron power,
And every man of sterling worth,
    Whose soul disdains to cringe, or cower
Beneath a haughty tyrant's nod,
And, supplicating, kiss the rod,
That, wielded by oppression's might,
Smites to the earth his dearest right,
The right to speak, and think, and feel,
    And spread his uttered thoughts abroad,
To labor for the common weal,
    Responsible to none but God—
Is threatened with the dungeon's gloom,
The felon's cell, the traitor's doom;
And treacherous politicians league
    With hireling priests, to crush and ban
All who expose their vile intrigue,
    And vindicate the rights of man.
How long shall Afric raise to thee
    Her fettered hand, oh Lord, in vain?
And plead in fearful agony,
    For vengeance for her children slain.

---

22. The poem also appeared in *Autographs for Freedom*, edited by Julia Griffiths (Boston: J. P. Jewett, 1853), a fundraising volume for *Frederick Douglass' Paper*.

23. Delany has the Cuban poet-revolutionary Placido speak the opening four lines of "How Long" in chapter 74 of *Blake*, right after he is attacked and injured in Havana by a white man from Baltimore. William Wells Brown prints an extract from the poem in his chapter on Whitfield in *The Black Man: His Antecedents, His Genius, and His Achievements* (1863).

I see the Gambia's swelling flood,
    And Niger's darkly rolling wave,[24]
Bear on their bosoms stained with blood,
    The bound and lacerated slave;
While numerous tribes spread near and far,
Fierce, devastating, barbarous war—
Earth's fairest scenes in ruin laid
To furnish victims for that trade,
Which breeds on earth such deeds of shame
As fiends might blush to hear or name.
I see where Danube's waters[25] roll,
    And where the Magyar[26] vainly strove,
With valiant arm, and faithful soul,
    In battle for the land he loved—
A perjured tyrant's legions tread
The ground where Freedom's heroes bled,
And still the voice of those who feel
Their country's wrongs, with Austrian steel.
I see the "Rugged Russian Bear"[27]
Lead forth his slavish hordes, to War
Upon the right of every State
Its own affairs to regulate:
To help each Despot bind the chain
Upon the people's rights again,
And crush beneath his ponderous paw
All Constitutions, rights and law.
I see in France, oh, burning shame!

24. The Gambia and Niger rivers are in West Africa, in areas that supplied many of the Africans brought to the Americas as slaves.

25. The Danube River flows through Hungary and Austria.

26. Hungarian. Whitfield alludes to the Hungarian Revolution of 1848–49, which was brutally suppressed by the Austrian leadership, working in alliance with Russia's Tsar Nicholas I.

27. A reference to Nicholas I, who was emperor of Russia from 1825 to 1855. The quotation comes from *Macbeth*, act 3, scene 4, when Macbeth addresses Banquo's ghost.

The shadow of a mighty name,[28]
Wielding the power her patriot bands
Had boldly wrenched from kingly hands,
With more despotic pride of sway
Than ever monarch dared display.
The Fisher,[29] too, whose world-wide nets
    Are spread to snare the souls of men,
By foreign tyrant's bayonets
    Established on his throne again,
Blesses the swords still reeking red
    With the best blood his country bore,
And prays for blessings on the head
    Of him who wades through Roman gore.
The same unholy sacrifice,
Where'er I turn, bursts on mine eyes,
Of princely pomp, and priestly pride,
    The people trampled in the dust,
Their dearest, holiest rights denied,
    Their hopes destroyed, their spirit crushed;
But when I turn the land to view,
    Which claims, par excellence, to be
The refuge of the brave and true,
    The strongest bulwark of the free,
The grand asylum for the poor
    And trodden-down of every land,
Where they may rest in peace secure,
    Nor fear th' oppressor's iron hand —

28. Louis Napoleon Bonaparte, president of the French Second Republic, whose government during 1848–52 became increasingly repressive and dictatorial. In late 1852, he named himself emperor of the Second Empire.
    29. A reference to the repressive Pope Pius IX, who temporarily surrendered power during the Roman Revolution of the late 1840s and then was restored to rule by the French and Austrians. "Fisher" alludes to Matthew 4:18–19, where Jesus refers to spiritual leaders as "fishers of men."

Worse scenes of rapine, lust and shame,
Than e'er disgraced the Russian name,
Worse than the Austrian ever saw,
Are sanctioned here as righteous law.
Here might the Austrian Butcher[30] make
    Progress in shameful cruelty,
Where women-whippers proudly take
    The meed and praise of chivalry.
Here might the cunning Jesuit learn —
    Though skilled in subtle sophistry,
And trained to persevere in stern,
    Unsympathizing cruelty,
And call that good, which, right or wrong,
Will tend to make his order strong —
He here might learn from those who stand
    High in the gospel ministry,
The very magnates of the land
    In evangelic piety,
That conscience must not only bend
    To every thing the Church decrees,
But it must also condescend,
    When drunken politicians please
To place their own inhuman acts
    Above the "higher law" of God,
And on the hunted victim's tracks
    Cheer the malignant fiends of blood;
To help the man-thief bind the chain
    Upon his Christian brother's limb,

30. Haynau [Whitfield's note]. Julius Jacob von Haynau (1785–1853) was an Austrian general known for his brutality in repressing revolutionaries in Italy, Hungary, and elsewhere. He was notorious for the public whippings he gave women who supported revolutionary causes; hence Whitfield's reference to "women-whippers."

And bear to Slavery's hell again
   The bound and suffering child of Him
Who died upon the cross, to save
Alike, the master and the slave.
While all th' oppressed from every land
Are welcomed here with open hand,
And fulsome praises rend the heaven
For those who have the fetters riven
Of European tyranny,
And bravely struck for liberty;
And while from thirty thousand fanes
   Mock prayers go up, and hymns are sung,
Three millions drag their clanking chains,
   "Unwept, unhonored and unsung;"[31]
Doomed to a state of slavery
   Compared with which the darkest night
Of European tyranny,
   Seems brilliant as the noonday light;
While politicians, void of shame,
   Cry, this is law and liberty,
The clergy lend the awful name
   And sanction of the Deity,
To help sustain the monstrous wrong,
And crush the weak beneath the strong.
Lord! thou hast said, the tyrant's ear
   Shall not be always closed to thee,
But that thou wilt in wrath appear,
   And set the trembling captive free;
And even now dark omens rise
   To those who either see or hear,

---

31. From Sir Walter Scott's *The Lay of the Last Minstrel* (1805), Canto Sixth, which depicts an exiled Scottish bard.

And gather o'er the darkening skies
   The threatening signs of fate and fear.
Not like the plagues which Egypt saw,[32]
   When rising in an evil hour,
A rebel 'gainst the "higher law,"
   And glorying in her mighty power—
Saw blasting fire, and blighting hail,
Sweep o'er her rich and fertile vale,
And heard on every rising gale,
Ascend the bitter, mourning wail;
And blighted herd, and blasted plain,
Through all the land the first-born slain,
Her priests and magi made to cower
In witness of a higher power,
And darkness, like a sable pall,
   Shrouding the land in deepest gloom,
Sent sadly through the minds of all
   Forebodings of approaching doom.
What though no real shower of fire
   Spreads o'er this land its withering blight,
Denouncing wide Jehovah's ire
   Like that which palsied Egypt's might;
And though no literal darkness spreads
   Upon the land its sable gloom,
And seems to fling around our heads
   The awful terrors of the tomb:
Yet to the eye of him who reads
   The fate of nations past and gone,
And marks with care the wrongful deeds
   By which their power was overthrown,

32. See p. 45, n. 6.

Worse plagues than Egypt ever felt
  Are seen wide-spreading through the land,
Announcing that the heinous guilt
  On which the nation proudly stands,
Has risen to Jehovah's throne
  And kindled his avenging ire,
And broad-cast through the land has sown
  The seeds of a devouring fire.
Tainting with foul, pestiferous breath
  The fountain-springs of moral life,
And planting deep the seeds of death,
  And future germs of deadly strife;
And moral darkness spreads its gloom
  Over the land in every part
And buries in a living tomb
  Each generous prompting of the heart.
Vice in its darkest, deadliest stains,
  Here walks with brazen front abroad,
And foul corruption proudly reigns
  Triumphant in the Church of God;
And sinks so low the Christian name,
In foul, degrading vice, and shame,
That Moslem, Heathen, Atheist, Jew,
  And men of every faith and creed,
To their professions far more true,
  More liberal both in word and deed,
May well reject, with loathing scorn,
  The doctrines taught by those who sell
Their brethren in the Saviour born,
  Down into slavery's hateful hell;
And with the price of Christian blood
Build temples to the Christian's God;
And offer up as sacrifice,
  And incense to the God of heaven,

The mourning wail, and bitter cries,
　　Of mothers from their children riven;
Of virgin purity profaned
　　To sate some brutal ruffian's lust,
Millions of Godlike minds ordained
　　To grovel ever in the dust;
Shut out by Christian power and might,
From every ray of Christian light.
How long, oh Lord! shall such vile deeds
　　Be acted in thy holy name,
And senseless bigots, o'er their creeds,
　　Fill the whole earth with war and flame?
How long shall ruthless tyrants claim
　　Thy sanction to their bloody laws,
And throw the mantle of thy name,
　　Around their foul, unhallowed cause?
How long shall all the people bow
　　As vassals of the favored few,
And shame the pride of manhood's brow,
　　Give what to God alone is due—
Homage, to wealth, and rank, and power
Vain shadows of a passing hour?
Oh for a pen of living fire,
　　A tongue of flame, an arm of steel,
To rouse the people's slumbering ire,
　　And teach the tyrant's heart to feel.
Oh Lord! in vengeance now appear,
　　And guide the battles for the right,
The spirits of the fainting cheer,
　　And nerve the patriot's arm with might;
Till slavery banished from the world,
And tyrants from their powers hurled,
And all mankind from bondage free,
Exult in glorious liberty.

THE ARCH APOSTATE[33]

"Since he miscalled the morning star,
Nor man, nor fiend hath fallen so far."—Byron[34]

WHEN gathered in the courts above,
    Before Jehovah's burning throne,
Archangels own his boundless love,
    And cast their crowns of glory down;[35]
While cherubim and seraphim,
    Thronging in serried ranks around,
Now raise on high the pealing hymn,
    And loud their Maker's praise resound;
Causing the arch of heaven to ring
With loud hosannas to their king.
And in a thousand varied lays
Pouring their raptured songs of praise,
A tribute to Almighty love,
Through which alone they live and move,
Praising the fixed, unchanging laws,
By which the first Eternal Cause
Propels the radiant spheres on high,
That through the illimitable sky
Pursue their never-varying course
Throughout the boundless Universe.

33. The poem first appeared in *Frederick Douglass' Paper*, 22 January 1852, 4, and addresses Massachusetts senator Daniel Webster (1782–1852), who voted to support the Compromise of 1850, with its Fugitive Slave Law (which required that all U.S. citizens return runaway slaves to their owners). An apostate is a person who forsakes his religion, cause, and party; for Whitfield, Webster was guilty of all three and thus embodied an evil analogous to that of Satan, particularly as depicted by John Milton in *Paradise Lost* (1667, 1674).

34. From "Ode to Napoleon Buonaparte" (1814), by Lord Bryon (1788–1824). The excerpt refers to the fall of Lucifer ("the morning star"; see Isaiah 14:12).

35. See Milton's *Paradise Lost*, book 3, lines 351–53.

And all the host to whom was given
　　The rays of bright intelligence,
To fit them for the joys of heaven,
　　Far higher than the carnal sense;
All owned the wisdom of those laws,
By which the first Almighty Cause,
Throughout Creation's vast expanse,
　　Imposed on every creature's mind,
Through endless ages to advance,
　　In good and evil unconfined:
That "higher law," which, fixed as fate,
Binds all of high or low estate.
But one, the foremost of that train,
　　The first in wisdom, power and might,
Who poured in heaven the highest strain,
　　And clearest saw both wrong and right,
Of loftiest, most capacious mind,
　　Of largest views, of strongest will,
Of power to dazzle, foil and blind,
　　Make evil good, and good seem ill,
With haughty and ambitious boast,[36]
　　To deeds of evil e'er inclined,
A third part of the heavenly host
　　Drew with him in rebellion blind;
And strove to make the lower law
　　Of his own lust, and hate, and pride,
The only source from whence to draw
　　For rules and precepts to decide;
And thus beneath his feet he trod
The statutes of Almighty God;

---

36. An allusion to Satan's oratorical power in *Paradise Lost*, as well as to that of the fallen angel Belial (see *Paradise Lost*, book 2, lines 112–15).

And by avenging justice fell
Down to the lowest depths of hell.
So in our Nation's Senate Hall,
     Where statesmen grave, in council meet,
By far the mightiest of them all,
     One called the Godlike, most complete
In all the attributes of mind,
That win the applause of human kind—
Whose learned thoughts, and glowing words,
In early days had oft been poured
In trumpet tones at Freedom's shrine,
And fanned the latent spark divine
Implanted in the human breast,
Of sympathy with the oppressed,
Into a bright and living blaze,
Beneath whose fierce and scorching rays,
Tyrants had cowered in the dust,
And slaves looked up with hopeful trust.
When Greece had broke the tyrant's chain,
     And bathed her sword in Moslem gore,
While Freedom's thrilling battle-strain,
     Was pealing o'er her classic shore,
His was the voice which, o'er the wave,
     Sent forth a loud and cheering note,
Aroused to strife the slumbering slave,
     And cheered the struggling Suliote.[37]
On Plymouth rock his voice was heard,[38]
In tones which like a clarion stirred

---

37. An inhabitant of the mountain area in northwestern Greece, known for resisting Ottoman rule and later participating in the Greek War of Independence against the Turks. Byron died in 1824 while participating in that war, which led to Greece's recognition as an independent nation in 1832.

38. In 1820, Webster delivered his famous "Plymouth Oration," which celebrated the liberty-loving Pilgrims who landed at Plymouth Rock in 1620.

The blood in every freeman's veins,
And caused the slaves on Southern plains,
To hail it as the harbinger
   Of bright and halcyon days to come,
When many a Northern Senator
   Shall dare to speak for those now dumb.
But oh, how changed![39] the giant mind
   That once had soared a Godlike flight,
And, 'mid the sceptered kings of mind
   Had mounted to the loftiest height,
Now prostrate, groveling in the dust,
Recreant to his most sacred trust,
The women-whippers' pliant tool,
   Perjured in sight of God and man,
And falsest of the hollow school
   Of demagogues, who lead the van,
The forlorn hope of slavery;
With intrigue, cunning, knavery,
Striving to quell the rising tide
   Of freedom setting o'er the land,
And threatening with tyrannic pride
   To all who dare for freedom stand,
The terrors of the dungeon's gloom,
The felon's cell, the traitor's doom;
Setting their own unholy laws
   Above the higher law of God;
Branding each one who scorns their cause,
   Nor fears the petty tyrant's nod,
A traitor, and an infidel,

39. Cf. Milton, *Paradise Lost*: "But O how fall'n! how chang'd / From him, who in the happy Realms of Light / Cloth'd with transcendent brightness didst outshine / Myriads though bright" (book 1, lines 84–87).

And hireling priests are paid to tell
    That those whom Jesus died to save,
And ransomed with his blood from hell,
    Were born to be their abject slaves;
And the rude rabble catch the yell,
And help the furious sound to swell,
Which sends a shout of joy through hell,
Where all the damned, in endless flame,
    Exult amid tormenting fire,
That men should take such pains to claim
    The notice of Almighty ire.
When all the deep-dyed villains come
To listen to their final doom,
And the great Judge himself portrays
    The different degrees of crime
Which marked their darkly devious ways,
    While passing through the rounds of time.
Arnold,⁴⁰ whose treacherous nature sought
    His country's freedom to betray,
For which himself had bravely fought,
    On many a doubtful battle-day;
And Gorgey,⁴¹ too, whose jealous spite,
    Betrayed his country to her foes,
And quenched in blood the dawning light
    That brightly o'er her prospects rose;
And Judas, who for paltry pelf,
    His Lord and Saviour basely sold,
And then, despairing, hung himself;
    And all, who, for the lust of gold,

---

40. Benedict Arnold (1741–1801), the American revolutionary who betrayed the cause in 1780 and took refuge in England.

41. The Hungarian military leader Artúr Görgey (1818–1916) was considered a traitor after he surrendered to Russian forces at Világos in 1849.

Or pride, or hate, or love of power,
   The tyrant or the traitor played,
Or faltering, in an evil hour,
   Their sacred trusts have all betrayed;
They yet shall scorn the proffered hand
Of him, the vilest of the band,
Who, having greater power of mind
   Than any other living man,
Had used it to debase his kind,
   And spread abroad the direst ban
Which man or devil ever saw,
Slavery's corrupt, inhuman law:
And, sinking from his high estate,
   Without excuse of any kind,
The lust of power, or pride, or hate,
   Or imbecility of mind,
Has stooped in Freedom's council halls,
   Where live the memories of the brave,
To be the meanest thing that crawls
   The earth—a voluntary slave.
In future years, when men desire
   To speak in strong hyperbole,
And give, in one small word, the fire
   And essence of iniquity—
That name shall suit their purpose well,
For not 'mid all the fiends of hell,
Could one be found that would express
So well, the depths of littleness;
And Webster's name shall ever be
The deepest badge of infamy.

THE MISANTHROPIST[42]

IN vain thou bid'st me strike the lyre,
　And sing a song of mirth and glee,
Or, kindling with poetic fire,
　Attempt some higher minstrelsy;
In vain, in vain! for every thought
　That issues from this throbbing brain,
Is from its first conception fraught
　With gloom and darkness, woe and pain.
From earliest youth my path has been
　Cast in life's darkest, deepest shade,
Where no bright ray did intervene,
　Nor e'er a passing sunbeam strayed;
But all was dark and cheerless night,
　Without one ray of hopeful light.
From childhood, then, through many a shock,
　I've battled with the ills of life,
Till, like a rude and rugged rock,
　My heart grew callous in the strife.
When other children passed the hours
　In mirth, and play, and childish glee,
Or gathering the summer flowers
　By gentle brook, or flowery lea,
I sought the wild and rugged glen
　Where Nature, in her sternest mood,
Far from the busy haunts of men,
　Frowned in the darksome solitude.
There have I mused till gloomy night,
　Like the death-angel's brooding wing,

42. First published in *Frederick Douglass' Paper*, 17 December 1852, 3.

Would shut out every thing from sight,
   And o'er the scene her mantle fling;
And seeking then my lonely bed
   To pass the night in sweet repose,
Around my fevered, burning head,
   Dark visions of the night arose;
And the stern scenes which day had viewed
   In sterner aspect rose before me,
And specters of still sterner mood
   Waved their menacing fingers o'er me.
When the dark storm-fiend soared abroad,
   And swept to earth the waving grain,
On whirlwind through the forest rode,
   And stirred to foam the heaving main,
I loved to mark the lightning's flash,
   And listen to the ocean's roar,
Or hear the pealing thunder's crash,
   And see the mountain torrents pour
Down precipices dark and steep,
   Still bearing, in their headlong course
To meet th' embrace of ocean deep,
   Mementoes of the tempest's force;
For fire and tempest, flood and storm,
   Wakened deep echoes in my soul,
And made the quickening life-blood warm
   With impulse that knew no control;
And the fierce lightning's lurid flash
   Rending the somber clouds asunder,
Followed by the terrific crash
   Which marks the hoarsely rattling thunder,
Seemed like the gleams of lurid light
   Which flashed across my seething brain,
Succeeded by a darker night,
   With wilder horrors in its train.

And I have stood on ocean's shore,
    And viewed its dreary waters roll,
Till the dull music of its roar
    Called forth responses in my soul;
And I have felt that there was traced
    An image of my inmost soul,
In that dark, dreary, boundless waste,
    Whose sluggish waters aimless roll—
Save when aroused by storms' wild force
    It lifts on high its angry wave,
And thousands driven from their course
    Find in its depths a nameless grave.
Whene'er I turned in gentler mood
    To scan the old historic page,
It was not where the wise and good,
    The Bard, the Statesman, or the Sage,
Had drawn in lines of living light,
Lessons of virtue, truth and right;
But that which told of secret league,
    Where deep conspiracies were rife,
And where, through foul and dark intrigue,
    Were sowed the seeds of deadly strife.
Where hostile armies met to seal
    Their country's doom, for woe or weal;
Where the grim-visaged death-fiend drank
    His full supply of human gore,
And poured through every hostile rank
    The tide of battle's awful roar;
For then my spirit seemed to soar
    Away to where such scenes were rife,
And high above the battle's roar
    Sit as spectator of the strife—
And in those scenes of war and woe,
A fierce and fitful pleasure know.

There was a time when I possessed
   High notions of Religion's claim,
Nor deemed its practice, at the best,
   Was but a false and empty name;
But when I saw the graceless deeds
   Which marked its strongest votaries' path,
How senseless bigots, o'er their creeds,
   Blazing with wild fanatic wrath,
Let loose the deadly tide of war,
Spread devastation near and far,
Through scenes of rapine, blood and shame,
Of cities sacked, and towns on flame,
Caused unbelievers' hearts to feel
The arguments of fire and steel
By which they sought t' enforce the word,
   And make rebellious hearts approve
Those arguments of fire and sword
   As mandates of the God of love—
How could I think that such a faith,
   Whose path was marked by fire and blood,
That sowed the seeds of war and death,
   Had issued from a holy God?
There was a time when I did love,
   Such love as those alone can know,
Whose blood like burning lava moves,
   Whose passions like the lightning glow;
And when that ardent, truthful love,
   Was blighted in its opening bloom,
And all around, below, above,
   Seemed like the darkness of the tomb,
'T was then my stern and callous heart,
Riven in its most vital part,
Seemed like some gnarled and knotted oak,
That, shivered by the lightning's stroke,

Stands in the lonely wanderer's path,
A ghastly monument of wrath.
Then how can I attune the lyre
   To strains of love, or joyous glee?
Break forth in patriotic fire,
   Or soar on higher minstrelsy,
To sing the praise of virtue bright,
Condemn the wrong, and laud the right;
When neither vice nor guilt can fling
   A darker shadow o'er my breast,
Nor even Virtue's self can bring,
   Unto my moody spirit, rest.
It may not be, it cannot be!
   Let others strike the sounding string,
And in rich strains of harmony,
   Songs of poetic beauty sing;
But mine must still the portion be,
   However dark and drear the doom,
To live estranged from sympathy,
   Buried in doubt, despair and gloom;
To bare my breast to every blow,
To know no friend, and fear no foe,
Each generous impulse trod to dust,
Each noble aspiration crushed,
Each feeling struck with withering blight,
With no regard for wrong or right,
No fear of hell, no hope of heaven,
Die all unwept and unforgiven,
Content to know and dare the worst
Which mankind's hate, and heaven's curse,
Can heap upon my living head,
Or cast around my memory dead;
And let them on my tombstone trace,
Here lies the Pariah of his race.

A HYMN,

WRITTEN FOR THE DEDICATION
OF THE VINE STREET METHODIST
EPISCOPAL CHURCH, BUFFALO[43]

GOD of our sires! before thy throne
    Our humble offering now we bring;
Deign to accept it as thine own,
    And dwell therein, Almighty King.
Around thy glorious throne above
    Angels and flaming seraphs sing,
Archangels own thy boundless love,
    And cherubim their tribute bring.

And every swiftly rolling sphere,
    That wends its way through boundless space,
Hymns forth, in chorus loud and clear,
    Its mighty Maker's power and grace.
It is not ours to bear the parts
    In that celestial song of praise,
But here, oh Lord! with grateful hearts,
    This earthly fane to thee we raise.

Oh, let thy presence fill this house,
    And from its portals ne'er depart;
Accept, oh Lord! the humble vows
    Poured forth by every contrite heart.

43. The Vine Street African Methodist Episcopal Church was founded in 1831 and had its first regular pastor in 1838. Located on Vine and Washington streets in a downtown area of Buffalo, the church became the site of a number of African American conventions and protests during the 1840s and 1850s. The National Convention of Colored Men was held there in 1843, and in 1850 it was the site of a major protest against the Fugitive Slave Law.

No sacrifice of beast or bird,
   No clouds of incense here shall rise,
But in accordance with thy word,
   We'll bring a holier sacrifice.

Here shall the hoary-headed sire
   Invoke thy grace on bended knee,
While youth shall catch the sacred fire,
   And pour its song of praise to thee.
Let childhood, too, with stammering tongue,
   Here lisp thy name with reverent awe,
And high, and low, and old, and young,
   Be brought t' obey thy holy law.

And when our spirits shall return
   Back to the God who gave them birth,
And these frail bodies shall be borne
   To mingle with their kindred earth—
Then, in that house not made with hands,
   New anthems to thy praise we'll sing,
To thee, who burst our slavish bands,
   Our Savior, prophet, priest and king.

YES! STRIKE AGAIN THAT SOUNDING STRING[44]

YES! strike again that sounding string,
    And let the wildest numbers roll;
Thy song of fiercest passion sing—
    It breathes responsive to my soul!

A soul, whose gentlest hours were nursed,
    In stern adversity's dark way,
And o'er whose pathway never burst
    One gleam of hope's enlivening ray.

If thou wouldst soothe my burning brain,
    Sing not to me of joy and gladness;
'T will but increase the raging pain,
    And turn the fever into madness.

Sing not to me of landscapes bright,
    Of fragrant flowers and fruitful trees—
Of azure skies and mellow light,
    Or whisperings of the gentle breeze;

But tell me of the tempest roaring
    Across the angry foaming deep,
Or torrents from the mountains pouring
    Down precipices dark and steep.

44. The poem appeared as "Yes! Strike Again that Sounding String!" in the *North Star*, 15 March 1850, 4. At the conclusion of her very favorable literary notice of *America and Other Poems* in the 15 July 1853 *Frederick Douglass' Paper*, Julia Griffiths, the English woman who was the managing editor of Douglass's newspaper, reprinted the poem, declaring that "the following lines forcibly remind us of BYRON. He who wrote them has verily the soul of a true poet, and should be taken by the hand by some of the more favored white bards to the land" (3).

Sing of the lightning's lurid flash,
   The ocean's roar, the howling storm,
The earthquake's shock, the thunder's crash,
   Where ghastly terrors teeming swarm.

Sing of the battle's deadly strife,
   The ruthless march of war and pillage,
The awful waste of human life,
   The plundered town, the burning village!

Of streets with human gore made red,
   Of priests upon the altar slain;
The scenes of rapine, woe and dread,
   That fill the warriors' horrid train.

Thy song may then an echo wake,
   Deep in this soul, long crushed and sad,
The direful impressions shake
   Which threaten now to drive it mad.

TO ——

APPROACHING night her mantle flings
   O'er plain and valley, rock and glen,
When borne away on fancy's wings,
   Imagination guides my pen.
I soar away to glittering spheres,
   And leave behind the sons of earth;
Lo! my enraptured fancy hears
   Seraphic strains of heavenly mirth.
A vision as of angel bright
   Sudden appears before my face,
A beauteous, fascinating sprite,
   Endowed with every charm and grace.

Majestic Juno's lofty mien,
    With beauteous Venus' form and face,
And chaste Diana's modesty,
    Adorned with wise Minerva's grace,[45]
United in thy form divine,
With most resplendent luster shine.
And when those matchless charms I viewed,
    Thy faultless form, and graceful mien,
Surprised, amazed, entranced I stood,
    And gazed with rapture on the scene.
And when thy lips were ope'd to speak,
    In tones so sweet, so soft and clear,
Gabriel[46] his golden harp might break,
    And seraphs lean from heaven to hear.
'T is the pure mind which dwells within,
    Displays itself in act and word,
And raises thee from every sin
    Far, far above the common herd.
And when the term of life is past,
    And thy pure soul returns to heaven,
The memory of thy worth shall last,
    While thought or mind to man are given.

45. On the various gods mentioned in this poem, see the notes to "To A. H." (nn. 12–20).
46. Biblical archangel who appeared to Daniel, Zacharias, and the Virgin Mary.

PRAYER OF THE OPPRESSED

OH great Jehovah! God of love,
    Thou monarch of the earth and sky,
Canst thou from thy great throne above
    Look down with an unpitying eye? —

See Afric's sons and daughters toil,
    Day after day, year after year,
Upon this blood-bemoistened soil,
    And to their cries turn a deaf ear?

Canst thou the white oppressor bless
    With verdant hills and fruitful plains,
Regardless of the slave's distress,
    Unmindful of the black man's chains.

How long, oh Lord! ere thou wilt speak
    In thy Almighty thundering voice,
To bid the oppressor's fetters break,
    And Ethiopia's sons rejoice.[47]

How long shall Slavery's iron grip,
    And Prejudice's guilty hand,
Send forth, like blood-hounds from the slip,[48]
    Foul persecutions o'er the land?

How long shall puny mortals dare
    To violate thy just decree,
And force their fellow-men to wear
    The galling chain on land and sea?

47. In the tradition of the Ethiopianism of Psalms 68:31 — "Ethiopia shall yet reach forth her hand unto God" — Whitfield here equates Ethiopia with Africa.
48. A type of leash from which dogs can be easily released.

Hasten, oh Lord! the glorious time
   When everywhere beneath the skies,
From every land and every clime,
   Paeans to Liberty shall rise!

When the bright sun of liberty
   Shall shine o'er each despotic land,
And all mankind, from bondage free,
   Adore the wonders of thy hand.[49]

TO S. A. T.

AS with thy Album[50] in my hand,
   Upon this picture late I gazed,
With tuneful harp held in its hand,
   And eyes of joy to Heaven upraised,
As if it inspiration sought
From Heaven's pure shrine of holy thought,
Like those inspired bards, who sung
Jehovah's praise with prophet tongue,
I thought of thee, as, long ago,
I heard thy voice so sweetly flow
Through measures of most tender feeling,
The soul of melody revealing;
Breathing, in sweetest harmony,
The noblest strains of poesy.
Like seraph of celestial fire,
Who tunes his voice and sacred lyre,

---

49. Delany reprinted the poem in chapter 61 of his novel, *Blake*, attributing it to the poet-rebel Placido, who recites it at the revolutionary Grand Council in Cuba.
50. A blank book into which were inserted drawings, favorite quotations, and autographs.

And moves th' angelic hosts above
To pour their notes of praise and love
To Him who sits enthroned on high
In undisputed majesty:
So thy harmonious notes divine
Cause men to bow before *thy* shrine;
Their adoration bring to thee,
Bright image of the Deity.

DELUSIVE HOPE[51]

IN the bright days of early youth,
 Hope told a fond, delusive tale
Of lasting friendship, holy truth,
 And steadfast love which ne'er should fail.
I listened to the flattering strain
 With all the fire of ardent youth;
And long I sought, but sought in vain,
 To find the dwelling-place of truth.
Though many in her garb appeared,
 Assumed her name and simple mien,
Ere long the vile deceit was cleared,
 And all the hypocrite was seen.
And friendship, too, though long and loud
 Her voice I've heard in many a place,
Among the fickle, thoughtless crowd,
 I never have beheld her face.
Love, next, its bright and glittering chain
 Around the captive fancy threw;

51. First published in *Frederick Douglass' Paper*, 12 November 1852, 4.

But soon its vows proved false and vain
    As the chameleons' changeful hue.
Now, when the hopes and joys are dead
    That gladdened once the heart of youth,
All the romantic visions fled
    That told of friendship, love and truth,
Turn we unto that steadfast friend
    Who guards our steps where'er they rove,
Whose power supports us to the end,
    Whose word is truth, whose name is love.

TO M. E. A.

OH! Had I that poetic lore
    Bestowed upon the favored few,
To ope' Dame Nature's bounteous store,
    And hold her treasures up to view,
To climb Parnassus' lofty mount,[52]
Or taste the Muses' sacred fount,
The far-famed Heliconian[53] spring,
Which Grecian poets erst did sing,—
And did Apollo,[54] and the Nine,
With eloquence and verse divine,
Direct my pen—I scarce could tell
The numerous charms which in thee dwell.
Thy loveliness of form and face
Might serve as model for a Grace;

52. In Greek mythology, Parnassus was a mountain in central Greece sacred to the gods.
53. Pertaining to Helicon, a mountain sacred to the nine Muses, from which sprang the fountains associated with poetic inspiration.
54. In Greek and Roman mythology, Apollo, the son of Zeus and Leto, is considered the god of light, truth, archery, and the arts.

And the bright luster of thine eye
Mahomet's Houris[55] far outvie.
The nobler beauties of the mind,
    Refined and elevated taste;
Great moral purity, combined
    With every outward charm and grace
And reason, governing the whole,
Displays in every act, a soul
High raised above the things which bind
Down to the earth more sordid minds;
And, soaring fetterless and free
In its unsullied purity,
Seems like a seraph wandering here,
The native of a brighter sphere.

A HYMN,

WRITTEN FOR THE DEDICATION
OF THE MICHIGAN STREET
BAPTIST CHURCH, BUFFALO[56]

ALMIGHTY God! in this thy house,
    For the first time thy people stand,
To pay to thee their humble vows,
    And crave fresh mercies at thy hand.
To thee, oh Lord! this house we rear;
    Deign thou the humble work to bless,
And grant that many souls may hear
    The words of truth and righteousness

---

55. See p. 52, n. 18.

56. Formally organized between 1832 and 1837, the Baptist Church of Buffalo was among the cultural centers of Buffalo's African American community, becoming a key stop on the Underground Railroad. The building itself was erected in 1849.

Which from thy servants' lips shall fall
  Who labor faithful in thy cause;
Oh may they hear and heed the call,
  And learn t' obey thy holy laws.
Here, often as thy saints shall meet,
  Deign thou to enter in the midst,
And guide our erring, wandering feet,
  In paths which lead to heavenly bliss.

Strengthen the wavering Christian's faith,
  Subdue the proud, exalt the meek,
Save sinners from eternal death,
  And lead us all thy truth to seek.
And when our humble prayers ascend,
  Hear thou, in heaven, thy dwelling-place;
O'er us thy guardian arm extend,
  And shed around thy heavenly grace.

And when the pealing hymn shall rise
  In strains of gratitude and praise,
Almighty monarch of the skies,
  Accept and bless our humble lays.
And when thy servants preach thy word,
  Thy Holy Spirit, oh, impart,
And make it like a two-edged sword
  Piercing to every sinner's heart.

And when the toils of life are o'er,
  · And these frail bodies turn to dust,
Receive us, Lord, forever more,
  Among the holy and the just.
Then, in that house not made with hands,
  We'll sing new anthems to thy praise,
To thee, who burst our slavish bands,
  And taught our hearts to love thy ways.

SELF-RELIANCE[57]

I LOVE the man whose lofty mind
   On God and its own strength relies;
Who seeks the welfare of his kind,
   And dare be honest though he dies;
Who cares not for the world's applause,
   But, to his own fixed purpose true,
The path which God and nature's laws
   Point out, doth earnestly pursue.
When adverse clouds around him lower,
   And stern oppression bars his way,
When friends desert in trial's hour,
   And hope sheds but a feeble ray;
When all the powers of earth and hell
   Combine to break his spirit down,
And strive, with their terrific yell,
   To crush his soul beneath their frown—
When numerous friends, whose cheerful tone
   In happier hours once cheered him on,
With visions that full brightly shone,
   But now, alas! are dimmed and gone!
When love, which in his bosom burned
   With all the fire of ardent youth,
And which he fondly thought returned
   With equal purity and truth,
Mocking his hopes, falls to the ground,
   Like some false vision of the night,
Its vows a hollow, empty sound,
   Scathing his heart with deadly blight,

57. The poem was first published as "Self Reliance" in the *North Star*, 14 December 1849, 4. Delany has the poet-revolutionary Placido recite a portion of the poem (as his own) in chapter 69 of *Blake*. According to the Oxford English Dictionary, the phrase "self reliance" was first used in 1833, eight years before the publication of Ralph Waldo Emerson's "Self-Reliance."

Choking that welling spring of love,
Which lifts the soul to God above,
In bonds mysterious to unite
The finite with the infinite;
And draw a blessing from above,
Of infinite on finite love.
When hopes of better, fear of worse,
   Alike are fled, and naught remains
To stimulate him on his course:
   No hope of bliss, no fear of pains
Fiercer than what already rend,
   With tortures keen, his inmost heart,
Without a hope, without a friend,
   With nothing to allay the smart
From blighted love, affection broken,
   From blasted hopes and cankering care,
When every thought, each word that's spoken
   Urges him onward to despair.
When through the opening vista round,
   Shines on him no pellucid ray,
Like beam of early morning found,
   The harbinger of perfect day;
But like the midnight's darkening frown,
   When stormy tempests roar on high,
When pealing thunder shakes the ground,
   And lurid lightning rends the sky!
When clothed in more than midnight gloom,
Like some foul specter from the tomb,
Despair, with stern and fell control,
Sits brooding o'er his inmost soul—
'T is then the faithful mind is proved,
   That, true alike to man and God,
By all the ills of life unmoved,
   Pursues its straight and narrow road.

For such a man the siren song
   Of pleasure hath no lasting charm;
Nor can the mighty and the strong
   His spirit tame with powerful arm.
His pleasure is to wipe the tear
   Of sorrow from the mourner's cheek,
The languid, fainting heart to cheer,
   To succor and protect the weak.
When the bright face of fortune smiles
   Upon his path with cheering ray,
And pleasure, with alluring wiles,
   Flatters, to lead his heart astray,
His soul in conscious virtue strong,
   And armed with innate rectitude,
Loving the right, detesting wrong,
   And seeking the eternal good
Of all alike, the high or low,
His dearest friend, or direst foe,
Seeks out the brave and faithful few,
Who, to themselves and Maker true,
Dare, in the name and fear of God,
To spread the living truth abroad!
Armed with the same sustaining power,
Against adversity's dark hour,
And from the deep deceitful guile
Which lurks in pleasure's hollow smile,
Or from the false and fitful beam
   That marks ambition's meteor fire,
Or from that dark and lurid gleam
   Revealing passion's deadly ire.
His steadfast soul fearing no harm,
   But trusting in the aid of Heaven,
And wielding, with unfaltering arm,
   The utmost power which God has given—

Conscious that the Almighty power
  Will nerve the faithful soul with might,
Whatever storms may round him lower,
  Strikes boldly for the true and right.

ODE FOR THE FOURTH OF JULY

ANOTHER year has passed away,
And brings again the glorious day
When Freedom from her slumber woke,
And broke the British tyrant's yoke—
Unfurled her standard to the air,
In gorgeous beauty, bright and fair—
Pealed forth the sound of war's alarms,
And called her patriot sons to arms!

They rushed, inspired by Freedom's name,
To fight for liberty and fame;
To meet the mercenary band,
And drive them from their native land.
Almighty God! grant us, we pray,
The self-same spirit on this day,
That, through the storm of battle, then
Did actuate those patriot men!

May those great truths which they maintained
Through years of deadly strife and toil,
Be by their children well sustained,
Till slavery ceases on our soil—
Till every wrong shall be redressed,
And every bondman be set free;
And from the north, south, east and west,
Paeans shall rise to Liberty.

May that same God whose ægis led
Our patriot sires on Bunker's[58] height,
Shed the same blessings on our head,
The heroes of a nobler fight—
A fight not waged by fire and sword,
And quenched in gore and human blood,
But only by that Sacred Word,
The mandate of Almighty God.

Our cause is Love, our weapon Truth,
Our ally is the living God;
Matron and maiden, sire and youth,
Shall feel the power of his rod.
Prone to the dust, shall Slavery fall,
And all its withering influence die,
While liberty, the boon of all,
Shall swell through earth, and air, and sky.

MIDNIGHT MUSINGS

THE gloomy night has cast a shroud
    Upon the dwelling-place of men;
Hushed are the voices of the crowd,
    And silence reigns o'er hill and glen.
My winged fancy takes its flight
    Through the unfathomed dark abyss,
And rends the vail of somber night
    From many scenes of woe and bliss.

---

58. The first significant military conflict between the colonial army and British forces, the Battle of Bunker Hill took place on 17 June 1775, in Charlestown, Massachusetts. Although the British troops emerged victorious, they suffered significant casualties, leading the colonists to claim a moral victory.

I enter first the poor man's cot;
   The sick wife, on her straw-made bed,
Reflects upon her lowly lot,
   While piercing pains distract her head;
The famished children's cries for bread
   Are issued in such piteous tones,
The father hangs his drooping head,
   To hear his wife and children's moans.[59]
The eyes of all that meager train
   Turned upon him to seek relief:
The thought o'erwhelms his burning brain
   With silent but expressive grief.
Near to the cot, a mansion proud
   Raises its stately roof tow'rd heaven;
While mirth and revelry full loud
   Burst on the stillness of the even.
Here wealth spreads her luxurious board,
   And glittering crowds the feast partake,
Not caring how the starving horde
   Of hungry poor their fast may break.
The wealth profusely squandered here,
   In gorgeous dress and proud array,
Would furnish forth good homely cheer
   On many a dreary winter's day,
To those who now, by want oppressed,
   Or smitten by some dire disease,
Pray fervently to God for rest,
   That death may come their pangs to ease.

---

59. A probable source (and subject) of the poem is Buffalo's 1849 cholera epidemic, which killed nearly 900 people.

And do you think a righteous God
    Will listen to your wretched pleas,
That when you saw his chastening rod
    Inflicting famine and disease
Upon your fellow-men, that ye
    Should grant no aid to their distress,
But use your every energy
    To wrong, and crush them, and oppress?
No! when you stand before his bar,
    You'll hear pronounced this awful doom:
"Depart from me, ye cursed, afar,
    And give my humble followers room!"

ODE TO MUSIC[60]

THERE's music wheresoe'er we roam—
'T is heard in ocean's crested foam,
And in the billows' deafening roar,
Which madly burst upon the shore:
They sing of Heaven's eternal Lord,
Who calms their raging by his word.

There's music in the gentle breeze,
Which softly blows among the trees,
Shaking fresh fragrance from the flowers,
In blooming fields and shady bowers;
They sing of Him whose power below,
Caused trees, and grass, and flowers to grow.

60. First published in the *North Star*, 22 March 1850, 4.

There's music in the numerous herds,
   Scattered about o'er hills and plains,
And in the flocks of feathered birds,
   Who, in a thousand varied strains,
Praise Him whose all-creating word
Brought into being beast and bird.

There's music in the tempest's sound,
   That darkly sweeps across the wave,
And hangs its shadowy pall around
   The ship-wrecked sailor's ocean grave;
Where the wild waste of waters yell,
Through caverns deep and dark as hell!

It speaks of His almighty power,
   Whose arm is ever stretched to save,
Who, in death's dark and trying hour,
   Can shed a halo round the grave;
And make the ocean's yawning cavern,
A glorious entrance into Heaven.

There's music in the thunder's roar,
   Which peals along the vault of heaven,
While torrents from the mountains pour,
   And trees by the dread bolt are riven;
Seen by the fiery element,
The earth, and sky, and sea seem blent.

It tells of Him whose wondrous power
   Can make the lightning do his will,
And sends the cool refreshing shower
   Upon the just and unjust still:
And whispers in a still, small voice,
To all the sons of earth, rejoice!

But leave this scene of doubts and fears,
   And swift on fancy's pinions fly,
And hear the music of the spheres
   Resounding sweetly through the sky;
They sing of Him, th' incarnate Word
Man's Saviour, Heaven's Almighty Lord!

Where'er we turn, music is found,
   With all its Heaven-born power to charm,
To lull us with its soothing sound,
   And shed around a holy balm—
Pure as the thrilling, heavenly strains
From angels' harps, on Judah's[61] plains.

Shall man, rescued from death and hell,
   Shall he alone refuse to raise
His feeble voice, the song to swell
   Unto his great Creator's praise?
While seraphs and archangels join
The blissful harmony divine.

Then let our tongues fresh music make,
   And sound his wondrous praise abroad;
And when the Universe shall quake,
   And Nature quail before her God,
We'll join the angels' choir above,
And sing our Lord's unchanging love.

---

61. Judah was an ancient kingdom in southern Palestine.

STANZAS FOR THE FIRST OF AUGUST[62]

FROM bright West Indies' sunny seas,
   Comes, borne upon the balmy breeze,
The joyous shout, the gladsome tone,
   Long in those bloody isles unknown;
Bearing across the heaving wave
The song of the unfettered slave.

No charging squadrons shook the ground,
   When freedom here her claims obtained;
No cannon, with tremendous sound,
   The noble patriot's cause maintained:
No furious battle-charger neighed,
No brother fell by brother's blade.

None of those desperate scenes of strife,
   Which mark the warrior's proud career,
The awful waste of human life,
   Have ever been enacted here;
But truth and justice spoke from heaven,
And slavery's galling chain was riven.

62. Great Britain abolished slavery in the West Indies on 1 August 1834. For African American abolitionists, the First of August was a day of celebration far more meaningful than July Fourth. Whitfield first presented this poem at a First of August celebration in Buffalo, which was described in an article in the *North Star*, 10 August 1849, 2. According to the reporter, the celebration concluded with an "Ode, written for the occasion, words by J. M. Whitfield," which was then reprinted as part of the article. Among those attending the celebration were the noted black abolitionists Charles Lenox Remond, David J. Peck, Henry Bibb, and Henry Highland Garnet. According to the *North Star*'s reporter, Whitfield offered two toasts at the close of the celebration: to Remond, for "his powerful advocacy of freedom in both hemispheres," and to "The Ladies, the only tyrants whose chains can be borne without resistance." The poem was reprinted on the front page of the 5 August 1854 issue of the *Provincial Freeman* shortly after the editors ran an admiring review of *America and Other Poems* in the issue of 15 July 1854, p. 2.

'T was moral force which broke the chain,
    That bound eight hundred thousand men;
And when we see it snapped in twain,
    Shall we not join in praises then?—
And prayers unto Almighty God,
Who smote to earth the tyrant's rod?

And from those islands of the sea,
    The scenes of blood and crime and wrong,
The glorious anthem of the free,
    Now swells in mighty chorus strong;
Telling th' oppressed, where'er they roam,
Those islands now are freedom's home.

THE NORTH STAR[63]

STAR of the north! whose steadfast ray
    Pierces the sable pall of night,
Forever pointing out the way
    That leads to freedom's hallowed light:
The fugitive lifts up his eye
To where thy rays illume the sky.

That steady, calm, unchanging light,
    Through dreary wilds and trackless dells,
Directs his weary steps aright
    To the bright land where freedom dwells;
And spreads, with sympathizing breast,
Her ægis over the oppressed.

63. Written for the North Star; a newspaper edited by a fugitive slave [Whitfield's note]. The poem first appeared in the *North Star*, 21 December 1849, 4. Douglass edited the *North Star* from 1847 to 1851, before changing the name of the paper to *Frederick Douglass' Paper*. Whitfield added the footnote for the 1853 republication in *America*..

Though other stars may round thee burn,
   With larger disk and brighter ray,
And fiery comets round thee turn,
   While millions mark their blazing way;
And the pale moon and planets bright
Reflect on us their silvery light.

Not like that moon, now dark, now bright,
   In phase and place forever changing;
Or planets with reflected light,
   Or comets through the heavens ranging;
They all seem varying to our view,
While thou art ever fixed and true.

So may that other bright North Star,
   Beaming with truth and freedom's light,
Pierce with its cheering ray afar,
   The shades of slavery's gloomy night;
And may it never cease to be
The guard of truth and liberty.

PART II Black Nationalism and Emigration

The letters, poems, and essays in Part 2 follow Whitfield over approximately two decades, beginning with a eulogy he delivered in 1841 on a fellow member of a black reading society in Buffalo and concluding with a letter he published in 1862 calling on the Union army to recruit black troops. The bulk of the materials in this section are from the 1850s, when Whitfield (now in his thirties) had become prominent among African Americans both as a poet and as an advocate for black emigration to Central or South America. We include in Part 2 the complete *Arguments, Pro and Con, on the Call for a National Emigration Convention* (1854), which has never before been reprinted and is one of the most revealing African American texts of the antebellum period. Much that was at stake for black leaders in the 1850s debate on black emigration can be gleaned from this document. *Arguments* reveals that Whitfield was a brilliant controversialist and political thinker who had no fear of debating Frederick Douglass and his associates and whose thoughts on blacks in the United States and the larger Americas may have had an important impact on Martin Delany's emigrationism. During this contentious period, Whitfield continued writing poems, some politically pointed (such as "The Vision") and some more personal and lyrical (such as "Morning Song"). In the two essays on black literary periodicals included here, Whitfield argues that blacks should attempt to achieve literary greatness by writing on topics not exclusively linked to race, politics, or nation. At the same time, the documents in this section demonstrate Whitfield's considerable interest in emigrationism, racism, black nationalism, and law. Even if we resist linking (or reducing) the poetry to the particular politics, say, of black emigration, we cannot ignore that Whitfield's poetry was written, read, and circulated in specific contexts of cultural debate and assumed some of its meanings from those contexts. The texts in Part 2 thus help to provide a broader picture of the cultural field in which Whitfield's work was emerging and circulating, though the question of how to read the poetry in relation to that field remains wide open.

Whitfield published *America* early in 1853 and dedicated the volume to Delany, who had publicly broken with Douglass to become the most prominent advocate of black emigrationism during the 1850s.[1] But despite his friendship with Delany, Whitfield demonstrated his political autonomy and savvy by attending Douglass's July 1853 Colored National Convention in Rochester, New York, which attracted a number of prominent black leaders, and serving on the committee of five that prepared and endorsed the convention's "Address, of the Colored National Convention, to the People of the United States." (Douglass was the main author.) The "Address" basically set forth Douglass's key positions of the time: the great value of Harriet Beecher Stowe's *Uncle Tom's Cabin* (1852) to the antislavery cause, the need for blacks to continue working for their economic uplift in the United States and to resist all emigrationist and colonizationist movements, the evils of the Fugitive Slave Law of 1850, and the moral imperative of fighting for black citizenship. As Douglass and the committee stated emphatically in the "Address": "We declare that we are, and of right we ought to be *American citizens*. We claim this right, and we claim all the rights and privileges, and duties which, properly, attach to it."[2]

The 1853 "Address" spoke in the spirit of numerous addresses and proclamations emerging from prior African American meetings. There are key similarities, for instance, between the "Address" and the resolutions adopted by an African American meeting in Cleveland that Whitfield had attended in 1838. But in the "Resolutions of the People of Cleveland, on the Subject of African Colonization," which the sixteen-year-old Whitfield helped to write, we see how even the young Whitfield was prepared to move in directions different from those of Douglass. Whitfield and his coauthors of the 1838 "Resolutions" declared their opposition to the project sponsored by the white leaders of the American Colonization Society of shipping the free blacks to the African colony of Liberia. But Whitfield and his associates saw clear distinctions between the colonization program of the society and the possibilities of black emigration, as suggested by one of the key resolutions adopted by the 1838 meeting: "*Resolved*, That we consider ourselves in the fullest sense, Americans, and entitled to all their rights, and if without crime, we must be banished, it should be our privilege to choose our place of banishment, which would be Hayti or Canada, rather than Liberia."[3] Whereas Douglass during the 1840s and 1850s saw little difference between colonization and emigration, Whitfield in 1838, and then during the 1850s, developed a hemispheric vision of "America" as offering possibilities for a black nationality beyond national borders, and a conviction that emigration differed considerably from colonization precisely because it was a matter of political choice.

Still, although the 1838 "Resolutions" point to a potential rift between Douglass and Whitfield, Whitfield shared much with Douglass about the importance of strengthening black community in the United States, which is no doubt why he attended Douglass's convention. A commitment to black elevation and an African American nationalism was absolutely central to Whitfield's abolitionist and antislavery work in Buffalo, where he participated in numerous black conventions, celebrations, and meetings from the late 1830s to the late 1850s, not one of which was specifically devoted to black emigration. Like Douglass, Whitfield emphasized the need for black literacy, as can be seen in the first document in Part 2, "Extracts from an Eulogy . . . upon the Life and Character of the Late Thomas Harris" (1841). In his tribute to the man who helped to form an African American reading association at the Buffalo library, Whitfield invokes the "dying injunctions" of Harris in order to underscore the close connections between "the proper improvement of the human mind" and blacks' "moral and political elevation." Whitfield makes similar arguments about African

American nationalism in his letter to Douglass of 30 August 1849, also included in Part 2, which supports Douglass's proposed National League as an organization that, like the Buffalo Library Association, would "draw out and embody the moral and intellectual power of the colored people of this country."

Whitfield may have shared Douglass's views on blacks' rights to U.S. citizenship and on the importance of black uplift and community, but soon after attending the Rochester convention, he began publishing letters attacking Douglass and his associate William J. Watkins for what he regarded as their accommodationism and political naiveté. Like Delany in his 1852 *Condition, Elevation, Emigration and Destiny of the Colored People of the United States*, Whitfield proposes in these letters, which are reprinted in *Arguments*, that blacks should consider emigrating from the United States to Central or South America because they currently are and seemingly forever will be disenfranchised by the white supremacist nation. Asserting in *Arguments*, as he had in the 1838 "Resolutions," that U.S. blacks would choose Haiti or Canada over Liberia, he lay claim to the American continent itself, arguing that emigration to Central and South America had the potential of bringing about the end of slavery by helping to create a formidable black nationality in close proximity to the U.S. nation. But in making such an argument, Whitfield risked reproducing the imperialism of white leaders of the time by representing African American emigration to the southern Americas as a form of "manifest destiny." As Whitfield elaborates in his letter of 25 September 1853: "I believe it to be the destiny of the negro, to develop a higher order of civilization and Christianity than the world has yet seen. I also consider it part of his 'manifest destiny,' to possess all the tropical regions of this continent, with the adjacent islands." Delany set forth a similarly providential (and hemispheric) racial nationalism eight months later in "Political Destiny," his lecture to the August 1854 emigration convention.[4]

Significantly, the literary remained central to both Douglass's and Whitfield's politics of black nationalism. Douglass may have attacked

Whitfield's politics, but he valued his poetry and continued to pub-
lish articles in *Frederick Douglass' Paper* praising his work. In September
1853, at a time when Whitfield had become highly critical of Douglass,
the anonymous author of "Our Literature" celebrated "the earnest en-
deavors which many individuals among us, such as James M. Whitfield
and Joseph C. Holly, are putting forth, in order to secure for them-
selves a position in the rank of authors." And in a speech printed in the
issue of 18 August 1854, William J. Watkins, the man who emerged as
Whitfield's primary opponent in the debate on emigration, devotes
the closing words of his August First West Indies Emancipation speech
to James Whitfield—"Let each one of us, then, unite in the fervent
aspirations of our own Whitfield"—and then quotes eight lines from
Whitfield's "How Long."[5]

The extent of Whitfield's poetry writing during this period re-
mains unclear. Because of their political disagreement on emigration,
he may have been reluctant to give his poetry to Douglass for publica-
tion. Nevertheless, the three Whitfield poems included in Part 2 were
published in *Frederick Douglass' Paper*, which suggests that Whitfield
and Douglass recognized their continued joint commitment to black
elevation. Other poems may have appeared in smaller-circulation
newspapers that are no longer extant or may have been written and
never submitted for publication. It is worth noting that none of the
published poems addresses emigrationism, and that only one of the
three has anything to do with politics. "The Vision," Whitfield's most
ambitious (and political) poem of the period, provides an apocalyptic
"vision" of humankind creating a hell on earth through the worship
of "Superstition." The poem has little to say about U.S. slavery and
virtually nothing about race and nation. Informed by his reading of
Milton's *Paradise Lost* and Byron's "The Dream," and perhaps by the
Puritan Michael Wigglesworth's apocalyptic "The Day of Doom,"
Whitfield uses the unrelenting iambic rhythms of the poem to convey
a global vision of the fall of humankind through the pursuit of power
and sensual gratification. The only "race" here is humanity itself:

> The human race shall all be found
> By stupid faith in senseless creeds,
> To perpetrate such guilty deeds,
> That Superstition shall go forth
> With War and Slavery through the earth. . . .

The concluding awakening of the poet from his nightmare vision hardly provides a reassuring sense of human, national, or racial possibilities. Instead, there is a foreboding Dickinsonian gloom: "And I in silence stood alone." Whitfield conveys a very different mood and perspective in "Morning Song," where he breaks from iambics, creatively works with enjambment, and conveys the connection between the poet and the Godhead in ways reminiscent of Emerson's "Bacchus." In Whitfield's other known poem of the period, "Lines, Addressed to Mr. and Mrs. J. T. Holly, on the Death of Their Two Infant Daughters," Whitfield, in the manner of Phillis Wheatley in her elegiac poems, adopts a ministerial voice in order to present the deaths of the daughters of a fellow emigrationist as signs that the girls had been chosen by God to escape the pains of life.

Whitfield's belief in the importance of literature to black uplift and community can be seen most explicitly in the document he produced for Delany's National Emigration Convention in Cleveland in 1854, "Report on the Establishment of a Periodical . . . ," and in the similar document he produced for the 1856 emigration convention, "Prospectus of the Afric-American Quarterly Repository." In these complementary texts, both of which are included in Part 2, Whitfield argues for the importance of black writing to black uplift, suggesting that blacks need a new journal that is not under the control of Douglass. Moreover, consistent with his interest in the larger Americas, his two calls for a journal of black writing speak to his hemispheric perspective on black nationalism, for he specifically seeks out Haitian and other writers from the southern Americas. Whitfield is also clear in not wanting the journal to be bound by politics. Although he says that antislavery writings will be part of his proposed "Afric-American

Quarterly Repository," he insists that the journal "will not be confined to this particular policy." Whitfield may have published one issue of the "Repository," but an extant copy has yet to be found.

Black emigrationism gained new momentum in 1857 after the Supreme Court ruled in the Dred Scott case that blacks never were and never could become U.S. citizens. James Theodore Holly and William Wells Brown promoted Haitian emigration, Delany began to think about African emigration, and Whitfield became intrigued by the plan proposed by Congressman Frank Blair of Missouri to use U.S. funds to purchase land in Central or South America for African Americans. In a speech to Congress of 14 January 1858, Blair called for the creation of a select committee to explore the possibility of such African American colonization. Although Blair lost the congressional election later in 1858, his ideas had broad appeal in the Republican Party, and he continued to champion his plan, gaining support among a number of black abolitionists who regarded it more as a program for emigration than for colonization. Blair gave a major address on the topic to the Mercantile Library Association of Boston on 26 January 1859, with Ralph Waldo Emerson in attendance. That talk was published as a pamphlet, with accompanying letters of support from black abolitionists, including Holly, Delany, and Whitfield. From Whitfield's perspective, such a colonization project would work against the desire of U.S. southerners to spread slavery into the southern Americas and, as Delany, Brown, and others elaborated, would help to develop a black nationality in the American hemisphere that would eventually challenge the southern slave power. As mentioned in the general introduction, there is evidence that during 1859–61 Whitfield considered emigration to Haiti and perhaps traveled across the Texas borderlands to explore the feasibility of Blair's plan, but all we know for certain is that he was in New Haven in 1860 and California in 1862.

Despite his initial support for Blair, Whitfield's views on black emigration clearly changed with the outbreak of the Civil War. Like most other advocates of emigrationism of the late 1850s and early 1860s, Whitfield saw the Civil War as a war of emancipation that promised to improve the prospects for blacks in the United States. In 1862, from his new home in California, he published a letter about the role that black troops could play in the Union cause, drawing on a long tradition of African American writing that saw blacks' participation in U.S. wars as establishing rights to citizenship. But even as Whitfield, Delany, and others who once supported black emigration increasingly embraced the possibilities of a U.S. nationalism that would include African Americans, Abraham Lincoln and his advisors proposed the possibility of colonizing the free blacks to Central America. Ironically, they supported their ideas about colonization by adducing Delany's emigrationist 1854 "Political Destiny" (which may have drawn from Whitfield's letters reprinted in *Arguments*) and a January 1862 petition from California blacks (signed by Whitfield) supporting Blair's colonization plan, both of which were reprinted by the House of Representatives in 1862.[6] Whitfield was not well known outside abolitionist circles, and yet, precisely because of his substantial cultural role, both his name and political ideas had found their way into Congress. By late 1862, Lincoln was moving in the very different direction that would culminate in his Emancipation Proclamation of 1 January 1863. Whitfield's hopes for and struggles with U.S. nationalism from his new location in northern California and elsewhere in the Northwest, particularly as expressed in his commemorative poetry, will be the focus of Part 3.

NOTES

1. From late 1847 to 1849, Delany had coedited the *North Star* with Douglass. By the early 1850s, however, the coeditors were expressing sharp disagreements on emigration, Harriet Beecher Stowe (Delany distrusted her), and a number of other issues. See Robert S. Levine, *Martin Delany, Frederick Douglass, and the Politics of Representative Identity* (Chapel Hill: University of North Carolina Press, 1997).

2. Frederick Douglass, J. M. Whitfield, et al., "Address, of the Colored National Convention, to the People of the United States," in *Proceedings of the Colored National Convention, Held in Rochester, July 6th, 7th and 8th, 1853* (Rochester: Frederick Douglass' Paper, 1853), 11.

3. "Resolutions of the People of Cleveland, on the Subject of African Colonization," *Colored American*, 2 March 1839, 1. (The article reprints an earlier article from

the *Cleveland Herald and Gazette*; the meeting itself occurred on 12 December 1838.) In *Arguments*, Whitfield claims to be one of the authors of the resolutions.

4. For instance, Delany declares that he sees "the finger of God" in noticing that the whites of the southern Americas have "*decreased* in numbers, *degenerated* in character, and become mentally and physically *enervated* and imbecile; while the blacks and colored people have studiously *increased* in numbers, *regenerated* in character, and have grown mentally and physically vigorous and active, developing every function of their manhood, and are now, in their elementary character, decidedly superior to the white race" ("Political Destiny of the Colored Race, on the American Continent," in *Proceedings of the National Emigration of Colored People; held at Cleveland, Ohio, on Thursday, Friday and Saturday, the 24th, 25th and 26th of August, 1854* [Pittsburgh: A. A. Anderson, 1854], 57).

5. "Our Literature," *Frederick Douglass' Paper*, 23 September 1853, 3; "Speech of Wm. James Watkins, Delivered on the First Day of August, at Columbus, Ohio," *Frederick Douglass' Paper*, 18 August 1854, 3. The author of *Freedom's Offering* (1853), a collection of antislavery poetry, Joseph C. Holly (1825–55) was the brother of James T. Holly and an opponent of emigration.

6. See U.S. House of Representatives, *Report of the Select Committee on Emancipation and Colonization* (Washington, D.C.: 1862), and *Memorial of Leonard Dugged, George A. Bailey, and other free colored persons of California, praying Congress to provide means for their colonization to some country in which their color will not be a badge of degradation* (Washington, D.C.: House of Representatives, 37th Congress, 2d session, Misc. Doc., No., 31, 1862). The *Memorial* was presented to Congress on 16 January 1862. Both James Whitfield and Joseph Whitfield signed the petition.

EXTRACTS FROM AN EULOGY DELIVERED BEFORE THE BUFFALO LIBRARY ASSOCIATION UPON THE LIFE AND CHARACTER OF THE LATE THOMAS HARRIS, BY J. M. WHITFIELD[1]

The document, of which the following extracts are but parts, came to hand in such a mangled state, from the manner it which it was mailed, as to render it impossible for us to publish it entire. We therefore take such parts as bear upon the main object, and which escaped unhurt.[2]

MR. PRESIDENT:—We have met this evening to pay the last sad tribute of respect, to the worth of a deceased member of this Society,[3] the late Thomas Harris. It is to me, sir, a matter of deep regret, that this duty has not been consigned to abler hands than those of the humble individual who now addresses you, to some one capable of doing justice to the fine talents and many virtues which characterized him while living.

When we contemplate the close of life, the termination of man's career, the varying scenes which chequer the troubled course of his short life, the darkness and chaos which hang over the tomb, the many opinions, vague phantasies, and skeptical doubts in relation to a future state of existence, all tend to invest the death of a human being with

1. From the *Colored American*, 27 March 1841, 1.

2. In all likelihood, the prefatory comments are by Charles B. Ray (1807–86), who at the time was the sole editor and proprietor of the New York–based African American newspaper the *Colored American*.

3. The Buffalo Library Association, an African American reading society, was founded in the late 1830s. Whitfield's eulogy suggests that Harris (who remains obscure) was a key participant and leader. See Monroe Fordham, *A History of Bethel A.M.E. Church, Buffalo, New York, 1831–1977* (Buffalo: Bethel History Society, 1978), 11. On the importance of black reading societies to black uplift, see Elizabeth McHenry, *Forgotten Readers: Recovering the Lost History of African American Reading Societies* (Durham: Duke University Press, 2002).

a mysterious and solemn influence upon the minds of men of reason. To-day man puts forth the tender bud of hope, to-morrow blossoms and bears his blushing honors thick upon him. The third day comes a killing frost, and consigns him, in the bloom of life, to a premature grave. With what care, then, should we employ every moment of the time allotted to us, in our short sojourn here, that when we are brought upon the bed of death, we can have the consoling assurance in a retrospection of our past life, that we employed the time as profitably as circumstances would permit.

The duties of man are many and arduous, commencing life the most helpless of animated creatures, by the power of his mind he soon teaches the brute creation to yield implicit obedience to his will, and as the powers of that mind expand, and its latent energies are developed, the character of the man is formed; and if those energies are guided by correct principles, enables him to approximate nearer and nearer, in a moral point of view, to the perfection of his great Creator. So was it with the individual whose loss we now deplore. Gifted by nature with superior talents, which he had taken great care to cultivate and improve, combining in an eminent degree, the vigor and energy of youth, with the wisdom and prudence of age, he was an example which all young men may be proud to imitate. Though exposed to all the vices which beset young men, in every city of any magnitude, he resisted all temptations with the firmness of a stoic. His life was a pattern of strict morality, probity and virtue, and in his death a family has lost one of its worthiest members, and society one of its brightest ornaments. His loss will be deeply deplored by every one who had the honor of his friendship, for to know him was to respect and esteem him in the highest degree. And when the time arrived in which the vital spark was to quit its mortal abode, he expressed that confidence, that resignation to the will of the omnipotent, which is an inseparable companion of a well spent life like his. But while we pour forth the manifestations of sorrow over the deceased, let us not forget that we have our duty as men to perform. Often during his illness, did he inquire about the association, and expressed a strong desire that it might go on and prosper. It remains for us to see that wish fulfilled. His discerning mind perceived that an association of this kind was one of the best, perhaps from the peculiar circumstances in which we are placed, I may say, the very best that could be formed; for such is the pecuniary condition of the great mass of our people, that a collection of standard literary works can be obtained only by associating their means in this manner, and in its public debates it furnishes a wide field for mental improvement, which cannot be obtained by us elsewhere, in consequence of that unjust and blighting prejudice, which withholds from us our inalienable rights, and withers all our energies.

-|-|-

Would all our young men but follow the example of him who has been so recently removed from among us, in resisting all the alluring baits to draw them from the paths of rectitude and virtue, and persevere in the cultivation of their intellectual faculties, we should soon arise from that degraded situation in which we have been placed for centuries, to the highest pinnacle of fame. But, sir, such men as he was are rarely met with; we shall seldom look upon his like again. Let us, however, remember his dying injunctions, to uphold this Association, and every institution, which like it, tends to our moral or political elevation. And when we reflect upon our situation, how important do those admonitions appear; the victims of a prejudice, as severe and unrelenting as it is unjust, which paralyzes our energies, and cripples all our powers, robs us of the attributes of freedom and of man, and consigns one-fifth of the population of this country, to a state of hopeless bondage, it behooves us to make all the exertions in our power to rise from this debasing state of thralldom.

This Association has been formed for the moral, mental, and political improvements of its members, and what can be of greater moment than the proper improvement of the human mind—that which makes man the lord of the creation? Man is a creature whose character is formed almost entirely by education; he comes into the world the most helpless being of all animated creatures; none are so utterly incapable of self-preservation as the young infant. And whereas, all animals know by instinct their natural enemies and friends, man has to learn, by sad experience, on the instruction of others.

⁘

The human mind, how Godlike in its attributes, free and untrammelled in all its actions, it avouches its divine origin. The body may be incarcerated within the walls of a dungeon, loaded with chains, and lacerated with the whip, but the mind is beyond the reach of the tyrant's power, no walls can confine it, no fetters hold it in subjection.

In view of these facts, how important it is that the mind should be properly cultivated, and its latent powers brought into early and vigorous action. As the refiner melts the gold, separates it from the ore, purges it from the dross, and brings forth the polished and shining metal, so a virtuous education purges the mind of those debasing passions and savage barbarities, which, in a state of nature, obscure the nobler qualities of man.

⁘

While a community of people are in a state of ignorance, they are always corrupted and depraved, all sentiments of morality and religion, and all noble and generous feelings are driven from their hearts, and superstition takes their place, sacrificing its millions of deluded victims upon the altars of idolatry. For example, we will look into Hindoostan, where we see mothers casting their infants into the Ganges, widows burning themselves alive upon the funeral piles of their husbands, some throwing themselves into pots of boiling oil, others roasting themselves before slow fires, and thousands crushed to death under the ponderous wheels of Juggernaut.[4]

---

4. Whitfield draws on British colonial stereotypes of Hindus in northern India (Hindustan) to present Indians en masse as ignorantly desiring death as a sort of martyrdom. Derived from the Sanskrit, "Juggernaut" has come to refer to unstoppable or insurmountable forces and has sources in a festival of the same name in which

⁘

We, three millions of the descendants of Africa, in this enlightened country, find ourselves in the most abject state of slavery that ever any people were placed in, from the first creation of the world down to the present time. Of all the systems of tyranny ever established by man, none can compare for a moment with American slavery. In its pernicious influence, both upon the master and the slave, we look in vain upon the annals of history to find a parallel to the oppressions we endure in this boasted land of liberty and equal rights, which styles herself, with lofty emphasis, "The land of the free and the home of the brave," the asylum of the oppressed, but from beneath this beautiful mask of liberty, the hideous features of the monster tyranny, are seen in all their horrid deformity, from which even the tyrannic Russian and the despotic and barbarous Turk, turn with horror and indignation.

And now, sir, while we have such a striking example before us of the uncertainty of human life, and how liable we are at any moment to be called away, may we so regulate our conduct, that we too may be ready to meet the summons without regret. And dispensing with those idle pleasures and frivolous amusements which benefit neither mind nor body, but tend to enervate and destroy both, turn our attention to the cultivation of that part of our being which shall survive unhurt, "the war of elements, the wreck of matter, and the crush of worlds."[5]

Hindu devotees of Krishna, according to the British, threw themselves under chariots in order to gain salvation. "Ganges" is the Anglicized name for the 1,560-mile river that flows through Hindustan.

5. From the play *Cato* (1713), by the English writer Joseph Addison.

LETTER TO FREDERICK DOUGLASS,
30 AUGUST 1849[6]

Buffalo, N.Y. Aug. 30, 1849

MR. EDITOR:—I was highly pleased to see in the North Star of the 10th, your plan for a National League.[7] The necessity of such an organization, to draw out and embody the moral and intellectual power of the colored people of this country, is too obvious to need argument. Through the medium of such an organization we can manifest to the people of this country, that we have sufficient capacity to understand and appreciate our rights, and the ability and spirit to maintain them.

The general outline of your plan I think unexceptionable, with the exception of the 7th Article, relating to the time and place of holding the annual meetings.[8] If a permanent place is to be appointed, it should be more central; certainly not farther east than Buffalo or Rochester. It is evident that it would be as unjust to the western people to select New York or Philadelphia, as it would be to the eastern people to choose Chicago or Cincinnati. With regard to the time, I think the first of August[9] the best period that could possibly be selected, for

6. From the *North Star*, 7 September 1849, 2.

7. In the 10 August 1849 issue of the *North Star*, Douglass printed an article, "The Union of the Oppressed for the Sake of Freedom," that called for a "National League" of "the free colored people." Arguing that African Americans would be much more effective in their opposition to slavery and pursuit of black elevation if they were "largely and effectively united," he proposed a constitution with fourteen articles. In article 3, he stated the large aims of the proposed national organization: "The object of the National League shall be, the abolition of slavery, and the elevation and improvement of the free colored people of the United States" (2).

8. Douglass suggested alternating meetings between New York City and Philadelphia.

9. As noted in relation to Whitfield's poem "Stanzas for the First of August," August First, the day of the 1834 emancipation of the slaves in the British West Indies, was adopted by many African American communities and abolitionists of both races as a day of celebration.

several reasons. The latter part of July, and the first of August is con-
sidered the dullest period of the whole season, for all kinds of business
except farming; so that of course, the majority of persons could attend
with less inconvenience then, than at any other time; and no day could
be selected more appropriate for an oppressed and outraged people to
assemble and devise plans for obtaining their just rights, and elevat-
ing their moral and intellectual character, than that on which nearly
a million of their brethren were raised from a state of chattlehood to
the full enjoyment of the rights and privileges of freemen. The annual
celebration of West India Emancipation for 1850 has been appointed
at Buffalo,[10] and will probably be attended by large numbers; and I
would suggest the propriety of calling a convention for the purpose
of organizing the League, at the same time and place.

Yours for Union and Freedom.

J. M. WHITFIELD

ARGUMENTS, PRO AND CON, ON THE CALL
FOR A NATIONAL EMIGRATION CONVENTION

[The complete text that follows presents a debate on black emigra-
tion between Frederick Douglass and William Watkins, on one side,
and James Whitfield, on the other, much of which took place in the
pages of *Frederick Douglass' Paper* beginning almost immediately after
Douglass's Rochester Colored National Convention of July 1853. In
response to Martin Delany's call in August 1853 for a National Emigra-
tion Convention of Colored People to be held in Cleveland, Douglass
and his associate William Watkins expressed their opposition, pre-
senting the movement as detrimental to their ongoing efforts at black

10. The 1850 date and place was affirmed at Buffalo's most recent celebration; see
"First of August Celebration at Buffalo," in the *North Star*, 10 August 1849, 2.

elevation in the United States. From Whitfield's and Delany's perspective, *selective* black emigration to Central and South America would make a strong political statement against whites' antiblack racism and help to develop a black nationality beyond the borders of the United States. For the most part, Douglass controlled the debate through his newspaper, and he eventually stopped printing Whitfield's letters. In *Arguments*, black supporters of emigration like M. T. Newsom (the publisher), James Holly (who wrote the introduction), and Whitfield attempt to take control from Douglass by giving the final word to Whitfield and the various emigrationists who provide information in the appendix. That said, Douglass and Watkins have an important place in the text, for their letters are reprinted as they first appeared in *Frederick Douglass' Paper*. One of the great virtues of *Arguments*, then, is that it displays both sides of a key debate in African American intellectual culture during the 1850s. It also displays Whitfield's talent for polemic and political argumentation.]

ARGUMENTS, PRO AND CON, ON THE CALL FOR A
NATIONAL EMIGRATION CONVENTION, TO BE HELD
IN CLEVELAND, OHIO, AUGUST, 1854, BY FREDERICK
DOUGLASS, W. J. WATKINS, & J. M. WHITFIELD. WITH
A SHORT APPENDIX OF THE STATISTICS OF CANADA
WEST, WEST INDIES, CENTRAL AND SOUTH AMERICA

PUBLISHED BY M. T. NEWSOM

Tribune Steam Presses:
GEORGE E. POMEROY & CO.,
TRIBUNE BUILDINGS, DETROIT
1854

INTRODUCTION

The following pages, containing arguments *pro* and *con* on the subject of the migration of the colored people of the United States to some point without their territory, for the purpose of establishing a Black nationality, are from the pens of F. Douglass and W. J. Watkins,[11] against the project, and J. M. Whitfield in favor. The articles of the former appeared as editorials in Fred. Douglass' paper, soon after the issuing of the call for a National Emigration Convention, by Delany, Webb, Bias,[12] and others; and those of the latter as letters in reply to the strictures on the call, contained in the articles of the former. The disputants are undoubtedly among the ablest to be found on either

11. During the 1850s, Frederick Douglass (1818–95) resisted all emigration movements. A machinist and teacher who was active in the antislavery movement, the Baltimore-born William J. Watkins (ca. 1826–?) shared Douglass's views and moved from Boston to Rochester in 1853 to become associate editor of *Frederick Douglass' Paper*.

12. During the early to mid-1850s, Whitfield and Delany were the most prominent supporters of black emigration. William Webb (1812–68), an ordained African Methodist Episcopal clergyman, met Delany in Pittsburgh and helped him to organize the 1854 Cleveland convention. The Philadelphia black abolitionist and temperance advocate James J. Bias (d. 1860) also supported the cause.

side of the question, and their productions are well worthy of the attention of the large mass of the colored people scattered throughout the United States, whose destiny is so ably discussed.

The subject is one of the most momentous that ever claimed the consideration of any people; and it is peculiarly interesting to the colored Americans in the present crisis of their development; and their future condition for weal or woe depends upon how they shall meet and decide upon this great question.

The year 1853 must form a remarkable epoch in the history of the Africo-American race in the United States. The National Convention of colored freemen, which assembled in Rochester July 6, 7, 8, of that year, presented one of the grandest arrays of talent and wisdom that ever assembled on this continent; and to them we are indebted for an informal national organization of a denationalized people, whereby an organic, though premature and sickly birth was given to the idea of national independence, and the command of national resources to elevate an oppressed and down-trodden people. This was the formation of a national council of the colored people. This imperfect evidence of fruitfulness in national resources scarce had time to speed on the electric wires to gladden the anxious hearts of millions who were in suspense, waiting on the deliberations of that convention, before a new conception was announced, that, happily, progresses in embryo with evident signs of hopeful delivery. This was the issuing of the call for the emigration convention that is to meet in Cleveland, Ohio, August 24, 25, 26, 1854, and in relation to which the following controversy has taken place.[13] These are the events that must render the year 1853 ever memorable in the annals of colored American destiny.

13. See *Proceedings of the Colored National Convention, Held in Rochester, July 6th, 7th and 8th, 1853* (Rochester: Frederick Douglass' Paper, 1853), and *Proceedings of the National Emigration Convention of Colored People; held at Cleveland, Ohio, on Thursday, Friday, and Saturday, the 24th, 25th and 26th of August, 1854* (Pittsburgh: A. A. Anderson, 1854).

This discussion in the public presses devoted to our interest was opportune, and every conceivable exertion should be made to scatter papers and documents containing the same broadcast over the land wherever a member of our race is situated. Too much praise, therefore, cannot be awarded to Rev. Matthew T. Newsom,[14] for his exertions to place it in the present pamphlet form for circulation.

The public mass of our people, whom time and opportunity will not allow to grasp, by their own mental effort, a clear and comprehensive view of the subject, will be able to do so, assisted by the brilliant elucidations of those distinguished controversialists.

In order to add to the practical character of this pamphlet, an appendix is subjoined, embracing some slight information of the various places proposed for emigration.

The result of the general circulation of this pamphlet during the six or seven months that yet precedes the time for the assembling of the Cleveland convention must produce a salutary effect upon its determination. With this hope, I cheerfully recommend it to the public generally, particularly to all colored Americans, for their patronage and perusal.

J. THEODORE HOLLY[15]
Detroit, Jan. 9, 1854

14. Newsom was a Detroit cleric and publisher; his biography remains obscure.

15. A champion of black emigration and an ordained Episcopal priest, James Theodore Holly (1829–1911) emerged by the late 1850s as the most prominent supporter of African American emigration to Haiti. His best-known work, *Vindication of the Capacity of the Negro Race for Self-Government and Civilized Progress* (1857), celebrates the black revolutionaries who helped to establish Haiti as an independent black republic in 1803.

ARGUMENTS,
PRO AND CON, ON THE CALL FOR A
NATIONAL EMIGRATION CONVENTION

CALL FOR A NATIONAL EMIGRATION CONVENTION
OF COLORED MEN, TO BE HELD IN CLEVELAND, OHIO,
ON THE 24TH, 25TH, AND 26TH OF AUGUST, 1854[16]

Men and Brethren:—The time has now fully come, when we, as an oppressed people, should do something effectively, and use those means adequate to the attainment of the great and long desired end—to do something to meet the actual demands of the present, and prospective necessities of the rising generation of our people in this country. To do this, we must occupy a position of entire equality of unrestricted rights, composed in fact, of an acknowledged necessary part of the ruling element of society in which we live. The policy necessary to the preservation of this element must be in our favor, if ever we expect the enjoyment of freedom, sovereignty, and equality of rights anywhere.

For this purpose, and to this end, then, all colored men in favor of emigration out of the United States, and opposed to the American Colonization scheme of leaving the Western Hemisphere,[17] are requested to meet in CLEVELAND, OHIO, on TUESDAY the 24th DAY of AUGUST, 1854, in a great NATIONAL CONVENTION, then and there, to consider and decide upon the great and important subject of emigration from the United States.

16. Beginning in August 1853, the Call was printed regularly in *Frederick Douglass' Paper* and other African American newspapers.

17. The American Colonization Society was founded in December 1816 with the goal of shipping the free blacks to Africa. To that end, the society established the colony of Liberia in Africa in 1822. The white founders thought of themselves as moderate reformers who beneficently wished to return blacks to their "natural" home, but abolitionists such as William Lloyd Garrison, Frederick Douglass, and many others regarded the colonizationists as racists intent on denying blacks their rights to U.S. citizenship.

One of the leading measures of the Convention will be, to appoint a competent commission to Central, South America and the West Indies, whose duty it shall be to obtain all the necessary information relating to these countries, and report thereon, according to the instructions of the Convention.

There will also be established, a permanent Board of National Commissioners, who shall have full power to take cognizance of, and the management of all matters pertaining to the great subject of Emigration.

No person will be admitted to a seat in the Convention, who would introduce the subject of emigration to the Eastern Hemisphere — either to Asia, Africa, or Europe — as our object and determination are to consider our claims to the West Indies, Central and South America, and the Canadas. This restriction has no reference to personal preference, or individual enterprise; but to the great question of national claims to come before the Convention.

All persons coming to this Convention must bring credentials properly authenticated, or give verbal assurance to the Committee on Credentials — appointed for the purpose — of their fidelity to the measures and objects set forth in this call; as the Convention is specifically called by, and for the friends of emigration, and NONE OTHERS, and no opposition to them, will be entertained.

The question is not whether our condition can be bettered by emigration, but whether it can be made worse. If not, then, there is no part of the wide universe, where our social and political condition are not better than here in our native country, and nowhere in the world as here, proscribed on account of color.

We are friends too, and ever will stand shoulder to shoulder by our brethren, and all true friends in all good measures adopted by them, for the bettering of our condition in this country, and surrender no rights but with our last breath; but as the subject of emigration is of vital importance, and has ever been shunned by all delegated assemblages of our people as heretofore met, we cannot longer delay, and will not be farther baffled; and deny the right of our most sanguine friend or dearest brother, to prevent an intelligent enquiry into, and the carrying out of these measures, when this can be done, to our entire advantage, as we propose to show in Convention—as the West Indies, Central and South America—the majority of which are peopled by our brethren, or those identified with us in race, and what is more, destiny on this continent—all stand with open arms and yearning hearts, importuning us in the name of suffering humanity to come, to make common cause, and share one common fate on the continent.

The Convention will meet without fail, at the time fixed for assembling, as none but those favorable to emigration will be admitted; therefore no other gathering may prevent it.

The number of delegates will not be restricted—except in the town where the Convention may be held—and their number will be decided by the Convention when assembled, that they may not too far exceed the other delegations.

The time and place fixed for holding the Convention are ample; affording sufficient time, and a leisure season generally—and as Cleveland is now the centre to all directions—a good and favorable opportunity to all who desire to attend. Therefore, it may reasonably be expected that this will emphatically, be the greatest gathering of the colored people ever before assembled in Convention in the United States.

Colonizationists are advised, that no favors will be shown to them or their expatriating scheme, as we have no sympathy with the enemies of our race.

All colored men, East, West, North and South, favorable to the measures set forth in this call, will send in their names (post paid) to M. R. Delany, or Rev. Wm. Webb, Pittsburgh, Pa., that there may be arranged and attached to the call, five names from each State.

We must make an issue, create an event, and establish a position for ourselves. It is glorious to think of, but far more glorious to carry out.

PITTSBURG, PA.

REV. WILLIAM WEBB,
M. R. DELANY,
H. G. WEBB,
THOMAS A. BROWN,
JOHN JONES,
R. L. HAWKINS,
SAMUEL VENERABLE,
JOHN WILLIAMS,
A. F. HAWKINS,
S. W. SANDERS,
JEFFERSON MILLER,

PHILADELPHIA, PA.

J. J. GOULD BIAS, M.D.,
A. M. SUMNER,
JOHNSON WOODLIN,
FRANKLIN TURNER,
JACOB B. GLASGOW,

ALLEGHENY, CITY.

REV. A. R. GREEN,
P. L. JACKSON,
P. H. MAHONEY,
G. HARPER,
JONATHAN GREEN,
H. A. JACKSON,
E. R. PARKER,
SAMUEL BRUCE,

NEW YORK.

JAMES M. WHITFIELD,
JOHN N. STILL,
STANLEY MATHEWS,
MOSES BURTON,

MICHIGAN.

REV. W. C. MUNROE,
WILLIAM LAMBERT,
REV. I. M. WILLIAMS,
REV. M. T. NEWSOM,
JAMES CAMPBELL,
JOHN FREEMAN,

INDIANA.

WILLIAM J. GREENLY,
JOHN CARTER,

CANADA.

HENRY BIBB,
J. THEODORE HOLLY,
E. D. CLAYBROOK,
A. W. CHANDLER,
HENRY CURTAIN,

CALIFORNIA.

HENRY M. COLLINS,
JOSHUA B. DELANY,
PETER BLACKSON,
HENDERSON NICHOLS,
WILLIAM HENRY REED.

DOUGLASS' REVIEW OF THE CALL[18]

We have no sympathy with the call for this convention which we publish in another column. Whatever may be the motives for sending forth such a call, (and we say nothing as to these) we deem it uncalled for, unwise, unfortunate, and premature; and we venture to predict that this will be the judgment pronounced upon it by a majority of intelligent thinking colored men. Our enemies will see in this movement, a cause of rejoicing, such as they could hardly have anticipated so soon, after the manly position assumed by the colored National Convention held in this city. They will discover in this movement a division of opinion amongst us upon a vital point, and will look upon this Cleveland Convention as opposed in spirit and purpose to the Rochester Convention. Looked at from any point, the movement is to be deprecated.

Then the call itself is far too narrow and illiberal, to meet with acceptance among the intelligent. A Convention to consider the subject of emigration, where every delegate must declare himself in favor of it before hand, as a condition of taking his seat, is like the handle of a jug, all on one side! This provision of the call looks cowardly. It looks as if the Conventionists are afraid to meet the colored people of the United States on the question of emigration.

We hope no colored man will omit, during the coming twelve months, any opportunity which may offer to buy a piece of property, a house, lot, a farm, or anything else in the United States, which looks to permanent residences here. On account of any prospective canaan which may be spread out in the lofty imaginations of the projectors of this Cleveland Convention.

F. D.

18. Douglass printed this rejoinder in *Frederick Douglass' Paper*, 26 August 1853, 2.

J. M. WHITFIELD IN REPLY TO F. DOUGLASS[19]

Buffalo, Sept. 25th, 1853

FREDERICK DOUGLASS, ESQ, — *Dear Sir:*—I have noticed, in your comments upon the call for the convention of the friends of Emigration to be held at Cleveland, many severe, and, in my opinion, unjust strictures upon the movement; and as I have seen objections of a similar import raised by others, I desire, with your permission, briefly to answer some of them.

One of the prominent objections raised against us by yourself and others, is that while we have issued a call for a National Convention of the friends of Emigration, for the purpose of devising the best means of carrying into operation what we believe to be just and wise policy, that is, the concentration, as far as possible, of the black race in the central and southern portions of America, so that it may exercise its proper influence in moulding the destiny, and shaping the policy of the American Continent, and in securing a proper field for the full development of its own power and resources, and while that call is emphatically for the friends of the measure, and none others — we are assailed on all sides as though we had no right to issue such a call — a course which can be accounted for only on the ground that the assailants suppose that we are incapable of acting for ourselves, or of knowing our own wants.

You say that "whatever may be the motives for sending forth such a call," you "deem it uncalled for, unwise, unfortunate, and premature;" and you "venture to predict that the same judgment will be pronounced upon it by a majority of intelligent thinking colored men."

19. According to Floyd J. Miller (*The Search for a Black Nationality: Black Emigration and Colonization, 1787–1863* [Urbana: University of Illinois Press, 1975], 139 n. 6), Whitfield's first letter was printed in a possibly-no-longer-extant October 1853 issue of *Frederick Douglass' Paper*, and some later letters were rejected by Watkins. The letters that Watkins (and Douglass) refused to publish may have appeared in more regional black newspapers with relatively low circulations, such as the *Aliened American* and *Voice of the Fugitive.*

It may, perhaps, be a sufficient answer to this, to say that the signers of the call, (many of whom are men of cultivated minds, not accustomed to rash or hasty action upon important subjects) after mature deliberation and interchange of views are fully convinced that it is imperatively called for, eminently wise and timely, and if conducted with energy, cannot fail of being salutary in its influence. You also say "our enemies will see in this movement a cause of rejoicing, such as they could hardly have anticipated so soon, after the manly position assumed by the colored National Convention held in Rochester. They will discover in this movement, a division of opinion amongst us upon a vital point, and will look upon this Cleveland Convention as opposed in spirit and purpose to the Rochester Convention."

So far from rejoicing, I believe that our enemies will see as much greater cause for dreading the holding of the Cleveland than of the Rochester Convention, as a master would have greater reason for fearing the loss of the slave, who arms himself, and leaves his premises with the determination to be free or die, than he would the one who, after a few vain supplications, submits to the lash, and devotes the energies which should be employed in improving himself and his children, to building up the fortune of a tyrant, whose constant endeavor is to crush him lower in degradation, and entail the same hopeless condition upon his posterity. I suppose the purpose of the Cleveland Convention to be as much superior to that of the Rochester Convention, as deeds are superior to words—as strenuous efforts to obtain freedom, even if unsuccessful, are superior to whining or supplicating submission to slavery. The purpose of the Rochester Convention (for which it deserves great credit as a step, and that, too, an important one, in the right direction) was to endeavor to create a union of sentiment and action among the colored people, and, to give it efficiency, by forming a kind of national organization here, under the overshadowing influence of our oppressors.[20] I believe that movement

20. As mentioned in the introduction to Part 2, Whitfield attended the Rochester convention.

to be a good one, because it must ultimately lead *"intelligent think-ing* colored men" to the conclusion which many of us ignorant and thoughtless ones have arrived at intuitively—that is, that colored men can never be fully and fairly respected as the equals of the whites, in this country, or any other, until they are able to show in some part of the world, men of their own race occupying a primary and indepen-dent position, instead of a secondary and inferior one, as is now the case everywhere. In short, that they must show a powerful nation in which the black is the *ruling* element, capable of maintaining a respect-able position among the *great* nations of the earth; and I believe that the reflex influence of such a power with the increased activity that its re-action will excite in the colored people of this country, will be the only thing sufficiently powerful to remove the prejudices which ages of unequal oppression have engendered, unless the bleaching theory of Henry Clay should prevail,[21] and be carried into practice, by which the negro race in this country is to be absorbed, and its identity lost in that of the Caucasian—a consummation in my opinion not to be wished for. I believe it to be the destiny of the negro, to develop a higher order of civilization and Christianity than the world has yet seen. I also consider it a part of his "manifest destiny," to possess all the tropical regions of this continent, with the adjacent islands. That the negro is to be the predominant race in all that region in regard to numbers, is beyond doubt.[22] The only question is, shall they exercise the power and influence their numbers entitle them to, and become the ruling political element of the land in which they live? or shall they, as too many of our brethren in this country seem to be willing

21. Kentucky congressman Henry Clay (1777–1852) championed the American Colonization Society's efforts to ship free blacks to Africa and was one of the principal architects of the Compromise of 1850. Like a number of whites of the time, he feared racial mixture but believed that whiteness would eventually prevail over blackness.

22. Delany makes the same argument in his "Political Destiny of the Colored Race on the American Continent," which was the keynote address at the 1854 Cleveland con-vention; see *Proceedings of the National Emigration Convention of Colored People*, 56–57.

to do, tamely submit to the usurpation of a white aristocracy, naturally inferior to themselves in physical, moral, and mental power, and devote their lives to building up a power whose every energy will be wielded to crush them? If the Cleveland Convention gives, as we hope it will, a proper response to these great practical questions, its position will be as much more manly than that assumed by the Rochester Convention, as freedom is superior to slavery, or self-reliance to childish dependence on others.

To the charge that "our enemies will discover a division of opinion amongst us upon a vital point," I would answer, what if they do? All but bigots and fanatics know that there ever have been, and probably ever will be, divisions of opinions among men upon questions vitally connected with their temporal and spiritual welfare; and the more vital the question, the greater the difference of opinion, and the harder to reconcile conflicting views—consequently all reasonable men are willing to make allowances for honest differences of opinion, because they know that entire unanimity is to be expected only where tyranny on the one hand dictates, and servility on the other submits. The only opposition that I am able to discover, either in spirit or in purpose, to the Cleveland Convention, is, that it goes a step further in the same direction, and purposes to walk in the path which the Rochester Convention has pointed out. The child who has ventured to stand alone, must, of necessity, either step on or fall down again and crawl in the dust; and as we prefer walking forward, although it may be with feeble and tottering steps, in the path where freedom and glorious destiny beckon us on, to crawling again in dust at the feet of our oppressors, we think that we deserve praise rather than censure for the choice.

The last objection that you make to the call, that it "is illiberal and cowardly," because it excludes all but the friends of the measure, is too ridiculous to deserve serious comment. What would be thought of the Whig or Democrat who should bring serious charge against the opposite party, because they would not admit him as a delegate to their Conventions, with the right to vote on shaping the policy, and nominating the candidates of his opponents? It strikes me that such a claim would be regarded as transcendently impudent, were not its impudence surpassed by its absurdity, and I doubt very much whether his opponents could be brought to recognize the justice of such a claim, however willing or anxious they might be to discuss the question at issue between them. The friends of Emigration are *not* afraid to meet the colored people on that subject, but they choose to rest under the imputation of cowardice, sooner than *prove* themselves fools by admitting the avowed enemies of a measure, as the ones to devise ways and means for promoting its success. However, if the opponents of Emigration desire, we are ready and willing to discuss it, either in a Convention, if they choose to appoint one for the purpose, or through the press; and all that we ask is, that an equally fair hearing shall be allowed to each party. We apprehend, however, that anything like a fair discussion of the subject is not desired by the opponents of the measure; but that an attempt will be made to excite the prejudices of the people beforehand, by raising the cry of Colonization, Expatriation, &c. If any of our brethren have arguments addressed to our reason as men, by which they think they can convince us of the folly of our measures, or the wisdom of their own, we will endeavor to receive and reply to them in the same spirit; but if wholesale denunciations and misrepresentations are to take the place of facts and arguments, we must respectfully but firmly decline entering into any such controversy. Life is too short, and our foes too numerous and powerful, for us to waste our time wrangling with brethren because we differ in relation to the means necessary to promote the same great end which we have equally at heart—the elevation of our race.

We hope that our brethren that differ from us in opinion will do us the justice to believe that our position in favor of emigration is the result of no rash and hasty speculation, but of full and well-matured deliberation; and that, therefore, the stereotyped and commonplace objections raised by them have been thoroughly examined by us in all their bearings, without at all shaking our confidence in the wisdom and policy of Emigration. We wish it also to be understood, that we consider the line of argument usually pursued by the colonizationists and abolitionists, pro and con, in relation to Colonization or Emigration *en masse*, to be a tissue of nonsense on both sides—because contending for the practicability, or impracticability, of a measure which is absolutely impossible. We do not wish it to be supposed that we are so utterly ignorant of the laws which govern population, as to think that a nation or class of people scattered through all the ramifications of society, in a great and civilized nation like the colored people in the United States, ever did, ever will, or ever can emigrate *en masse*. No fact is better fixed in the world's history than this, that a people who have passed the pastoral state, never can by any possibility be brought to emigrate *en masse*. If our brethren will bear these things in mind, it may lead them to form a more correct opinion of our position than they seem to have done hitherto.

Respectfully yours,

J. M. WHITFIELD

W. J. WATKINS' REVIEW OF J. M. WHITFIELD

We call the attention of our readers to the letter of our esteemed friend, J. M. Whitfield, in reply to what he has pleased to designate our "*many* severe and unjust strictures" upon the Emigration movement.

We were not aware till the gentleman informed us, that we had commented *at length* upon the merits of the proposed Convention; and must express our surprise that any one should regard the article adverted to, which appeared in our issue of August 26th, as being characterized by a spirit of severity and injustice.

> "Optics sharp it needs, I ween,
> To see what is not to be seen."[23]

23. From John Trumbull's patriotic mock epic *M'Fingal* (1775–82), canto 1, lines 67–68.

If our friend had followed our example, so far as brevity is concerned, we should not have had *quite* so long a letter from his fruitful pen. The favors of our correspondents are always thankfully received, and respectfully solicited; especially if written in conformity with the *multum in parvo* principle.[24]

But to the letter. Mr. Whitfield takes umbrage at our declaration that we deem the call for the Convention uncalled for, unwise, unfortunate, and premature. The men of "sound and cultivated minds," to whom he adverts, "deem" otherwise. They, after "mature deliberation," are "fully convinced that it is imperatively called for." We were already advised, from the reading of the call, that none but those with certain predilections would be entitled to seats in this "*National*" Convention. We were not, however, apprised of what seems to be the fact, that we had committed a horrible thing by presuming to differ in opinion from these gentlemen of "sound and cultivated minds;" those whose "mature deliberation" is to elaborate some plan for "*moulding the destiny and shaping the policy of the American continent!*"

Mr. W. believes that our enemies will see great cause for dread in the holding of the proposed Convention, and institutes a comparison between the effects produced upon them by the position maintained by the Rochester Convention, and those likely to be produced by the contemplated one in Cleveland. Well, we have watched with eagle eye, the effect which the Convention in Rochester has had upon those, who, like Mr. W., apparently believe that the two races, so called, cannot live and move, and have their being together in this country. While they award us great credit for the ability displayed, the talent developed in the Convention, they all, with one accord, deplore our inflexible determination to continue struggling in the land of our birth, with that ardor, and resolution, and confidence in the inherent righteousness of our cause, which should characterize a people determined to be FREE. The fact is, colonizationists are resolved to drive us from the country. It matters but a very little to them *where* we go. We

24. "Much in little" (Latin).

must not stay *here*, infusing our deadly virus into the hearts of those
over whom the Juggernaut of Slavery rolls its ponderous weight. They
don't dread so much our emigration to the "West Indies, or Central
and South America, or the Canadas," as our *proximity to those of our
brethren who are in bonds*. We venture to predict that colonizationists
will interpose no barrier to the emigration of our people, should they
be so blind and infatuated, as to resolve not to be "*colonized*," O no! but
to "*emigrate*." 'Tis colonization after all, arrayed in the baptismal robe
of "emigration."

Our friend Whitfield speaks of the condition of the colored people
in this country as a "hopeless" one. Now, we believe in the efficacy, the
triumph of Truth. Truth is mighty and will prevail. If our confidence
was in an arm of flesh, we, too, would bid farewell to Hope. But our
confidence is in Him who maketh the clouds His chariot, and rides
upon the wings of the wind. Sorrow and darkness may continue for
a night, but joy shall come forth in the morning. God shall make the
wrath of man to praise Him, and the remainder of wrath will he re-
strain. It shall be so, for His own mouth hath spoken it. We intend to
"hope on, hope ever," believing that "God is just, and His justice shall
not sleep forever."[25]

We may talk morning, noon, and night, about "manifest destiny,"
and "shaping the policy of the American continent." The fact is, we
intend to stay *here* where God has placed us, and vindicate our dignity
as men. "We will plant our trees in American soil and repose in the
shade thereof." Horace Greeley[26] is right when he says it is settled that

25. In Query 18 of his 1785 *Notes on the State of Virginia*, Thomas Jefferson imagines
the possibility of the slaves rising up against their oppressors and proclaims, "I tremble
for my country when I reflect that God is just: that his justice cannot sleep forever"
(*The Works of Thomas Jefferson*, ed. Paul Leicester Ford [New York: G. P. Putnam's
Sons], 4:84).

26. Following the adoption of the Compromise of 1850, Horace Greeley (1811–72),
the well-known editor of the *New York Tribune*, emerged as a powerful voice against
slavery. Whitfield, who moved to California in the early 1860s, may have been in-
spired by his famous call, "Go West, young man, go West."

we are here among the whites, and intend to stay. Yes! we will remain, and not "tamely submit to the lash," as our friend W. intimates, but "fight the good fight of faith," believing that God will yet declare concerning us, as of His oppressed people of old: "I have seen the affliction of my people, and am come down to deliver them."[27] Heaven haste the auspicious era! We might review our friend W's article more closely, but, to use his own language, "life is too short, and our foes too numerous and powerful, for us to waste our time in wrangling with brethren because we differ in relation to the means necessary to promote the same great end which we have equally at heart, the elevation of our race."

W.

WHITFIELD IN ANSWER TO WATKINS[28]

Buffalo, N.Y., November 15, 1853

MR. EDITOR,

Nothing can be more unpleasant than to differ in opinion upon important points from those for whom we entertain the highest respect and the kindest affection; but when, by such persons, our position is perseveringly misunderstood, it is no more than just that we should claim the privilege of correcting such misrepresentations; and if, in such case, the much in little, (*multum in parvo*) principle should be apparently neglected, it may be readily accounted for upon the ground that it is easier to make or deny charges than it is to substantiate or refute them. That you would not have been satisfied with such a summary disposition of your article as you made with the call, is evident from the peculiar umbrage given to you by the only portion of my letter in which such a disposition was made of any part of your ar-

27. See Exodus 3:7 and Acts 7:34.
28. The letter first appeared in *Frederick Douglass' Paper*, 25 November 1853, 3.

ticle, and that was the portion where you announced it to be, in your opinion, uncalled for, unwise, unfortunate, and premature; and I, in answer, quoted the well matured opinion of such men as Wm. Webb, J. J. G. Bias, M. M. Clark, M. R. Delany, Wm. Lambert, A. R. Green, H. Bibb, J. T. Holly, W. C. Munroe, A. M. Summer,[29] and others, supposing them to be worth as much on one side of a question, with which they are equally conversant, as those of F. Douglass and W. J. Watkins are on the other. In other words, that such men are capable of thinking and acting for themselves, especially upon questions vitally connected with their own interest, and to which their attention has been earnestly devoted for years. In your reply to my letter, you, rather disingeniously [*sic*], I think, try to convey the impression that you are attacked for presuming to differ in opinion from these gentlemen, when you very well know that the letter was called forth by your *severe* attack upon these gentlemen for presuming to differ in opinion from you. But you are unwilling to admit that you made many "severe and unjust strictures upon the emigration movement, or commented upon it at length." You must certainly be aware that in an article like the one in question, consisting of bare assertion, unsustained by facts or arguments, "the *multum in parvo* principle" may be carried to perfection, and without being lengthy, you can be both severe and unjust. We may differ in relation to what number may be denominated many, but I will arrange the charges in regular order, and ask you to substantiate them, or do not blame us for characterizing them as severe and unjust. 1. It is uncalled for. 2. Unwise. 3. Unfortunate. 4. Premature. 5. Will please our enemies. 6. It is ungentlemanly. 7. Opposed in spirit

29. A mix of well-known and relatively obscure participants in the black emigration movement of the early to mid-1850s. The former slave Henry Bibb (1815–54) published *Narrative of the Life and Adventures of Henry Bibb* in 1849, and in 1850 he fled to Canada and established the antislavery, emigrationist newspaper *Voice of the Fugitive*, which published some of Whitfield's writings. The Reverend William C. Munroe ran a school for blacks in Detroit, which Bibb briefly attended in 1842. Munroe remained an important leader among African Americans in Detroit and had a key role in the 1854 Cleveland convention.

and in purpose to the Rochester Convention. 8. Narrow and illiberal. 9. Cowardly.

In my former letter I remarked that probably the opponents of emigration did not desire anything like a fair discussion of the question, but would endeavor to excite prejudice beforehand, by raising the cry of colonization, expatriation, &c.; and the result shows that my expectations were well founded, for you inform your readers that "'Tis colonization after all arrayed in the baptismal robes of emigration." It matters but little to us what name you give us, so long as you do not misrepresent our position.

You speak of my calling the condition of the colored people in this country hopeless, and draw the inference that I "do not believe that the two races can live, and move, and have their being together in the country;" I would ask you to carefully look over my letter again, and see if there is anything in it to justify such remarks. What are the fundamental points laid down in that letter as the basis of any discussion on the subject? 1st, That the mass of colored people in this country must ever remain here, and never can by any possibility be brought to emigrate *en masse*; and that, therefore, the stereotyped arguments on the practicability, or impracticability, of an *en masse* emigration, are a tissue of nonsense on both sides, and unworthy a moment's consideration. 2nd, That the tendency of political events is towards the formation of a great nation, or family of nations, occupying the tropical regions of this continent and its islands, in which the black is to be the predominant race, at least in numbers; and that true policy requires that it should be rendered so politically, as well as numerically. 3d, That the reflex influence of such a power, with the increased activity which its reaction will excite in the coloured people in this country, will be the only thing sufficiently powerful to remove the existing prejudice, unless the bleaching theory should prevail in practice, and the Negro race be absorbed, and its identity lost in the Caucasian. A consummation which our bitterest enemies, however much they may oppose it in theory, are striving with all their might to reduce to practice, and which every friend of liberty and morality should endeavor to prevent. It must be evident to every one, that the brotherhood and equality of mankind cannot be vindicated by a process, which leaves an oppressed and degraded class at the mercy of the brutal lust of their oppressors, until by an unlimited system of concubinage, steadily pursued for ages, the differences of race and color are lost, and the heterogeneous mass becomes moulded into a homogenous people — nor by one race occupying everywhere a secondary and dependent position, while the other occupies a primary and independent one — but full and fair equality can be looked for, only through the existence of national organizations of the different races, each occupying the same manly, independent, self-governing position. Then, and not until then, can amalgamation, or social intercourse, take place without disgrace to either party; but in the present condition of the races, all such amalgamation, or social intercourse, must be conducted in such a manner as to be shameful and humiliating in the utmost degree, to the proscribed class. Yet we have men among us, who, on general subjects, evince sufficient intelligence and self-respect, men that act as leaders of the people, who when colored conventions are called, to labor for the rights which have been wrested from us, or colored institutions are proposed, for the purpose of enabling colored youth to obtain some of the facilities for instruction so unjustly withheld from them, while so liberally awarded to the whites — condemn such conventions and institutions as being proscriptive, not from excluding white men from equal participation in their privileges, but for not giving a special invitation to the class who have cast us out from among them with contempt, and would hardly shake hands with us with a pair of tongs. With just as much reason might the beggar in his wretched hovel be accused of proscription, who should sit down to his meagre repast without sending a special invitation to the wealthy banker who would kick him out of doors if he attempted to enter his premises to share it with him.

You say that "colonizationists are resolved to drive us from the country, and care but very little where we go. That they don't dread so much our emigration to the West Indies, or Central or South America, or the Canadas, as our proximity to those of our brethren who are in bonds;" and declare your intention to remain here where God has placed you. Did you really mean what you wrote then? I think not. Let us examine and see. God has placed you in Maryland, right by the side of your "brethren in bonds," where you could remember them as being bound with them in the most literal sense. Why did you not remain in that *proximity*, instead of going to Massachusetts and New York? Was it not because in spite of that proximity you found you could not help yourselves, much less your "brethren in bonds;" and by removing to a free *State* you could do more to elevate yourselves and improve your own condition, and as a necessary consequence to benefit your brethren also? If such be the case, why should you censure us for following out the same logical deductions a step farther, and drawing the conclusion that we can exercise a greater influence for bettering the condition of ourselves, and our enslaved brethren by moving into a free *nation* than we can by remaining in a slaveholding one; especially when our proximity to our brethren in bonds will be no wise diminished thereby; for if either Canada, the West Indies or Central America be chosen, particularly the two latter, we shall be at least as near to the mass of our "brethren in bonds" as you will be in Rochester. Our enemies are not so ignorant as not to see that the existence of an independent community of negroes upon their southern frontier, is a dangerous example to be held out to their slaves; hence their threats of going to war if necessary to prevent the abolition of slavery in Cuba—their machinations to foment discord in and prevent the growth and prosperity of Hayti—and their systematic attempts to spread erroneous impressions relative to the efforts of emancipation in the British and French islands. They also see that the surest way of keeping the negroes down is to prevent their concentration, as much as possible, when they might learn to know and respect each other, and become acquainted with their own strength and resources, and keep them "scattered and peeled," "meted out and trodden down" in their midst, constrained to engage in the lowest and most menial occupations, and by the pressure of circumstances around them deprived of the power of acting with energy and efficiency or unitedly upon any subject; and to turn the course of those who may be disposed to emigrate towards Africa, where it will be impossible for them to exert the same influence upon slavery here, that they would if located in the West India islands, or the adjacent parts of the continent. In accordance with this policy we see that they are ready to go to war or at least to threaten it, for the purpose of preventing the abolition of slavery in Cuba, (which would secure negro ascendancy there,) and at the same time are willing to pay $100,000,000, for the purpose of admitting Cuba into the Union, where the whole power of this great confederacy can be wielded to crush the black, and keep him forever in a state of servile dependence upon the white.[30]

It is rather amusing to see the course pursued by the enemies of this movement; public meetings and individuals have expressed their opinion in sorrow, or in anger, according the mood of the different persons; yet not one of them have ventured to attack any of the positions laid down by us, but each erects his man of straw, names him Emigration Movement, and fires away at him with all his might. Mr. David Jenkins of Columbus, Ohio, in a letter to the *Aliened American*, works himself up into a perfect frenzy;[31] and in language similar to that of the New York *Herald*, when stirring up the ruffians of that city

30. During the 1840s and 1850s, the U.S. government explored various possibilities of obtaining Cuba. These efforts gained added currency as governmental policy with the Ostend Manifesto of 1854, in which U.S. diplomats declared that "Cuba is as necessary to the North American republic as any of its present members, and that it belongs naturally to that great family of states of which the Union is the Providential Nursery." Much of the acquisition effort was led by proslavery leaders, who hoped to link U.S. slavery with slavery in Cuba. Slavery was not abolished in Cuba until 1886. The term "manifest destiny," which presented U.S. expansionism as a providential imperative, was in all likelihood first used by John Louis O'Sullivan (1813–95) in an essay titled "Annexation," published in the July and August 1845 issues of the *United States Magazine and Democratic Review*.

31. The African American newspaper *Aliened American* was established in 1853 in Cleveland but lasted less than a year. The editor, William Howard Day (1825–1900),

to mob anti-slavery meetings, calls on the people of Cleveland not to suffer the Convention to be held there. He may rest assured that the Convention will be held. A public meeting also held at Columbus, over which the same gentleman presided, informs us that it "no longer sees us as friends, but inveterate enemies and haters of the cause we once advocated;" and invokes "shame and indignation" upon us. The answer to these brethren is that in whatever light they may see us, we shall continue to be, as we have been heretofore, the staunch friends of every thing in our judgment calculated to promote the elevation of our race, and the uncompromising enemies of everything which, in our opinion, tends to degrade it. Many of the signers of that call have entertained for years the same opinion of the policy of emigration which they now advocate. The writer of this article at least, (and I may say the same of several others,) has entertained the same opinion from boyhood, and time has but served to strengthen his convictions. The first article I ever wrote for publication was as Chairman of a Committee appointed by a meeting of the colored citizens of Cleveland, held in the winter of 1838–9 to prepare an address on the subject of emigration, recommending a concentration upon the borders of the United States, having particular reference to California.[32] That address was adopted, nearly or quite, unanimously by the meeting, and published in some of the papers; and was assailed on all sides with the fiercest animosity. I have lived to see men who ridiculed the idea of going to California, to build up the country, and be possessors and owners of the soil, the makers of its laws, and controllers of its destiny; after waiting until white men have gone in and possessed the soil, and made laws to degrade the negro below the level of the brute,

---

attended Douglass's 1853 Rochester convention but then broke with Douglass to support Whitfield's and Delany's emigrationism. David Jenkins (1811–77), who supported Douglass's anti-emigrationism, edited the Ohio abolitionist newspaper *Palladium of Liberty*, which he established in 1843.

32. The "Resolutions of the People of Cleveland, on the Subject of African Colonization" appeared in the 2 March 1839 issue of the *Colored American*.

while welcoming the men of every other race and nation—after all this, you can see these same men flocking in crowds to California, to perform the menial services of white men, and no warning voice is heard from any of our mentors, probably because they are satisfied with that state of things, as one to which they are accustomed. To see the white independent, the black dependent; the white filling the high, the black the low positions of society; the white making and executing the laws, the black not allowed to testify in a court of justice; in short the white the master, the black the servant. If such a course as this is pursued, what stronger proof could be desired by our enemies in support of their favorite argument, that the negro is incapable of self-government, and aspires no higher than to be a servant to the whites.

You say that your "trust is not in an arm of flesh, but in Him who maketh the clouds His chariot, and rides upon the wings of the wind; that He is just, and His justice shall not sleep forever;" and express your belief that "He will yet declare concerning us, as of His oppressed people of old, I have seen the afflictions of my people, and am come down to deliver them." Did you mean to carry out the parallel to its full extent, and intimate that He will deliver us "as He did His oppressed people of old," by bringing us out in a body, "with a high hand, and with an outstretched arm?" If so, you are greater emigrationists than I am. I too have implicit faith in the justice of the same Almighty Being, and that faith is none the less strong because I believe that in the natural world He works by natural means, and uses arms of flesh to work out His own Omniscient purposes, or to use your own words, in another column of the same paper, that He helps those who help themselves. To call upon the Lord to do that for us which we should perform ourselves, is but a solemn mockery, too much akin to the hypocritical cant of the pious knaves who defend slavery, with all its train of hellish abominations, as a Heaven-ordained institution, and traffic in the bodies and souls of men for the glory of God. What we have to do then, is to put our own hands to the plow, assured that if we do our share of the work, God will not fail to perform His; remembering that "who would be free themselves must strike the blow;" "and work out their own salvation."[33]

Respectfully yours,

J. M. WHITFIELD

WATKINS' FIRST REJOINDER[34]

November 25, 1853

Just before our paper was put to press, we accidentally caught a glimpse of the letter of this gentleman, being in the lecturing field at the time of its reception, and from which we have just returned.

The letter is written in a good spirit, and despite its exorbitant length, we cordially welcome it to our columns; at the same time we would remark that communications, from whatever source they may emanate, and however ably they are written, will prove more acceptable to our readers generally, if the ideas attempted to be conveyed, be not clothed in such interminable prolixity. Again, we would remark to our friend that we notice the fact that *his* letters are caught up with avidity, and published in the *Aliened American* and *Voice of the Fugitive*, and our *short responses* do not, somehow, find way into their columns.

Our friend finds fault with the "inference" which we consider the irresistible deduction of his own logic. He believes, then, that the two races can live, and move, and have their being together, in this country. But we would ask the plain question, does he not, in company with those whom he parades before the public as the heroes of the "Emigration" movement, maintain the position, that "colored men can never be fully and fairly respected as the EQUALS of the whites in

---

33. The quotations draw from Byron's *Childe Harold's Pilgrimage* (1818), canto 2, verse 76 (perhaps as adduced in Henry Highland Garnet's 1843 "Address to the Slaves of the U.S."), and Philippians 2:12–13.

34. The letter first appeared in *Frederick Douglass' Paper*, 25 November 1853, 2.

this country," and *therefore* they must leave the United States? Now, if they do not make this affirmation in so many words, their actions, which speak more loudly than words, certainly warrant such an interpretation of their position. If they believe with us, that by remaining *here*, and battling for the right, we shall evidently stand out in the sunlight on the broad platform of equality, why turn their backs upon the contest, and flee from the country under the pretext of "shaping the policy of the American continent?" We make the broad, unqualified assertion, that we regard any movement which contemplates the removal or emigration of the Free Colored People of these United States, to *any* land, near or remote, as a virtual endorsement of the fundamental principles which underlie the whole fabric of African Colonization. Colonizationists affirm that we can never in the United States rise superior to the adverse circumstances by which we are surrounded; that the color of our skin, the texture of our hair, and diversity of our physical conformation, preclude the possibility of our elevation here.

Mr. Whitfield declares that "the mass of the colored people in this country must ever remain here, and can never, by any possibility be brought to emigrate *en masse*."

Then what an egregious absurdity is the contemplated "Cleveland Convention?" For what purpose is the Convention called? Why, of course, to "consider and decide upon the great and important subject of emigration from the United States." Individual emigration? No! Not if words are the representatives of ideas. The call is for a *National* Emigration. National Emigration means emigration of the *nation*. This Convention is to be held, then, for the purpose of carrying out a measure which our friend himself declares to be "unworthy of a moment's consideration."

Again; Mr. W. informs us that "the tendency of political events is towards the formation of a great nation, or family of nations, occupying the tropical regions of this continent and its islands," &c. This may be so; but it by no means follows that it is *our* "manifest destiny" to become a member of this illustrious family. "Tropical regions, forsooth!" Now, we would seriously inquire of our Emigration friends, whether they are in earnest when they urge, among other consider- ations, as an objection to their abode in Africa, the "uncongeniality" of tropical climate. We know some men whose names are appended to the "Call," who have prated very loudly about the *fatal* folly which our people would exhibit, by leaving a climate *so congenial with our constitu- tion*, for one of sickness, devastation, and death; or, in other words, the exchanging of a temperate for a torrid zone. When they are urged to emigrate to Africa, they cry out "No, we can't live in a *tropical* clime." Now, so far as this family of nations is concerned—this family that is destined to occupy the "tropical regions," we fancy that the *very few* who will leave the States—would hardly come up to the idea of a *na- tion*. We believe with Mr. W., that it is our manifest destiny to remain *here*, and this opinion is based upon a limited knowledge of the laws which govern population.

Then let the nations occupy, if they please, the tropical regions of this continent, or any other; and if the reflex influence of such a power will remove existing prejudices against us in this country, then with all our hearts, we exclaim, Amen!

The remainder of this gentleman's letter will be considered at a future period. We consider this Cleveland Convention movement as one affording aid and comfort to the enemy. We do not believe the men whose names are appended to this Call, seriously contemplate emigration. No: they will meet in public Convention, and adopt a long series of resolutions, then return to their homes, and *stay* there. *They* will not leave the country, neither will *we*. And we here inform them, and all others concerned, that unless they show to our people more convincing evidence of *their* intention to leave the country, we shall henceforth regard them as insincere in the theory they promul- gate. When these men leave the country, may we be there to see. This Emigration question is an important one, and we have no disposition to pass it lightly by, but consider the work of our elevation HERE, as one of transcendent importance, and shall act accordingly; and we cannot understand why gentlemen so well-informed as Messrs. Whitfield and Delany, can consent, for a moment, to occupy a position which obviously confounds them with that despondency which has ever embarrassed and clogged the wheels of our efforts at elevation in the United States. And we call upon them in the name of our already too deeply bowed down people to drop their Emigration Scheme, and put their shoulders to the wheel of the first national car of the colored people ever set in motion in these United States.

w.

WATKINS' SECOND REJOINDER[35]

We have since our last issue, re-perused the letter of Mr. Whitfield, and carefully weighed its contents. Before entering upon its merits or demerits, we have a word to say to our readers. We wish it distinctly understood, that the proclivity of some men to enter the arena of conflict, is something wholly foreign to our nature. We have seen people who were like the troubled sea, unless an opportunity favorable to the development of their warlike propensities, continually presented itself. This was one of the leading characteristics of the *bellique* Cæsar. "Never mind, brother Toby," he would say, "by God's blessing, *we shall have another war break out again*, some of these days, and when it does, the belligerent powers, if they would hang themselves, cannot keep *us* out of play."[36]

We lay not the flattering unction to our souls, that we possess a particle of Cæsar's *courage*. We do not voluntarily and cheerfully leap into the gladiatorial arena; but, if forced thither, we will fight to the best of our ability, unless we can effect an honorable retreat.

These remarks are induced from a consciousness of the fact that too many of our leading men, or would-be leaders, apparently delight in

35. The letter first appeared in *Frederick Douglass' Paper*, 2 December 1853, 2.
36. From Laurence Sterne's *Tristram Shandy* (1760–7), vol. 6, chap. 31.

being submerged in the turbid waters of strife; but, amphibious–like, they can live also when ranging the pleasant fields of love and harmony. With these land and water men we have no sympathy. So far as Mr. W. is concerned, we make no personal allusion. We suppose him to be a gentleman of noble and generous impulses. We believe, also, that the policy he so ably advocates, is one which involves an admission detrimental to the interests of those to whom we are identified. We regard the ground-work of this theory radically defective. The emigration movement receives its vitality, if it has any, from assumptions which are untenable and gratuitous; and we shall contribute our humble quota toward the development of their fallacy.

First, then, those who advocate the policy of the Emigration of the Free Colored People of these United States to *any* country, we care not whether its locality be a desirable one on account of its proximity to the slave population, or otherwise, virtually admit the truthfulness of the position which Colonizationists assume, viz: *that our elevation in* THIS *country* is an absolute impossibility; that it is an incongruity wholly irreconcilable with the law of our destiny.

This is a most suicidal assumption, the correctness of which we are not yet willing to concede. We do not assert that our friend W. and others, admit the *righteousness* of that barbarous policy which mercilessly compels us to occupy a secondary position in this country. Certainly not. But, simply, that the very fact of our friends having called a Convention "to consider and decide upon the great and important subject of Emigration from the United States," proves, if it proves anything, that they have lost that faith which has hitherto nerved us onward, unparalleled by the terrific thunders of the wrath of man. Their prospects of the ulti-triumph of our heaven-born cause, have been quenched by the pitiless pelting of the storm.

Their action demonstrates their belief in the ultimate discomfiture of those, who cling with unyielding tenacity to those signs of the times, which we regard as auguring its final triumph. Here, then, really, is the point at issue. Not, exactly, as some of our friends would declare, whether or not our condition "can be made worse by Emigration," but whether or not we have implicit confidence in the ultimate success of the anti-slavery movement; *whether Might or Right shall triumph in the present conflict.* What, then, is the position which Emigrationists and Colonizationists assume? Whoever will take the pains to read the first paragraph of the Call for the Cleveland Convention, will readily discern that those who sympathise with it, regard their condition in this country as one from which they can, by no contingency, hope to emerge. "The time has now *fully* come when we, as an oppressed people, should do something effectively, and use those means adequate to the attainment of the great and long-desired end, to do something to meet the actual demands of the present and prospective necessities of the rising generation of our people in this country." Now, in order to effect this desirable consummation, what policy must be pursued? Must we remain here, battling in defence of our rights as men, implicitly relying upon the willingness, and ability, and intention, so to speak, of Jehovah, to crown our efforts with signal success? Not at all. What then? The idea of Emigration, is held out to our oppressed people as a "sovereign balm for every wound." To meet these "present demands, and prospective necessities, we must occupy a position of entire *equality*, and *unrestricted* rights," &c. For the purpose of attaining this equality and preparing for these "prospective necessities," all those in favor of "emigrating out of the United States," are invited to assemble in Cleveland, in Convention. Here is the position assumed: We can never be the equals of the whites in this country, and we must, therefore, prepare for our exodus.

This, we consider a most fatal admission, and one which, at *this crisis*, operates as mollifying ointment upon the gangrene heart of American Despotism.

Here, then, do we make the issue with Emigrationists. *They are confounded with that despondency and despair which preclude the possibility of their working for their elevation here, with that hopeful ardor which is the life-blood of the anti-slavery enterprise.*

We, who are opposed to Emigration, occupy a different position. In waging war with the enemy, and believing in the final triumph of the right, we do not believe that we are the victims of a miserable delusion. A contemplation of the past, and its contrast with the present, inspire us with confidence and hope for the future. We, therefore, intend to work faithfully and fearlessly, and hopefully, for our elevation HERE, till victory perch upon our banner.

Believing with Mr. W., that it is "*our manifest destiny to remain here,*" it is our respective duty, to march onward, in the path of progress, and look onward; and if it be the destiny of that "*family of nations* to occupy the tropical regions of this continent, and its islands," we, who are an integrant part of THIS nation, (though crushed and bleeding,) should, instead of preparing for our exodus to other lands, calmly and stoically suffer our hardship here, cordially awaiting the arrival of that auspicious era, when "the reflex influence" of that potent family, will "remove the existing prejudice against us" here.

We do not believe in herding ourselves together, in this country, or in any other. We will not *willingly* segregate ourselves from the rest of mankind. We are part and parcel of the *American Nation*. At any rate, we will join this tropical family, only as a *dernier resort*. If Slave-holders, and their apologists, succeed in driving us from the country; if our star of *Hope* go out in darkness, then we'll join this family, and not till then. This was the position of Frederick Douglass, in his Broadway Tabernacle Speech, May 11th, '53.[37] Said he,

"Sir, I am not for going anywhere. I am for staying precisely where I am, in the land of my birth. But, Sir, if I must go from this country; if it is impossible to stay here, I am then for doing the next best, and that will be to go wherever I can hope to be of most service to the colored people of the United States. Americans, there is a meaning in those figures I have read. God does not permit twelve millions of his creatures to live without the notice of his eye. That this vast people are tending to one point on this continent is not without significance.

37. "A Nation in the Midst of a Nation: An Address Delivered in New York, New York, on 11 May 1853." Douglass published the speech on the front page of the 27 May 1853 issue of *Frederick Douglass' Paper*.

All things are possible with God. Let not the colored man despair, then. Let him remember that a home, a country, a nationality, are all attainable this side of Liberia. But for the present the colored people should stay just where they are, unless where they are compelled to leave. I have faith left yet in the wisdom and justice of the country, and it may be that there are enough left of these to save a nation."

Again; neither Colonization, nor Emigration, is a remedy for the ills of the Colored American. He cannot emigrate from *himself*. He cannot destroy his own identity. If he leaves the country, he must carry his tastes and predilections with him. *If these are what they should be, he will here rise, superior to the adverse circumstances by which he is surrounded. If they are not, he will rise no where; but must ever occupy a degraded position.*

Our friend W. virtually accuses us of dishonesty, in uttering sentiments, which do not emanate from the heart. We stated in a former article on this subject, that Colonizationists are resolved to drive us from the country, and care but very little where we go. What they dread is, our proximity to our brethren in bonds. To prove we did not mean what we wrote, he triumphantly inquires "why we did not remain in Maryland, instead of going to Massachusetts and New York?"

Now, we reiterate our declaration, and would ask Mr. W., if he does not know it to be true? We might, had we time, adduce the speeches of the great leaders of the Colonization movement, in which this fact stands out in bold relief. They declare without reservation, that our presence in this country, exerts an unfavorable influence upon the Slave population. We render the slave discontented, and consequently, we must be driven from them. But friend W., suppose we did leave Maryland? What if we are not in contact with the Slave; does this fact prove the fallacy of our assertion? We are still in the country. When we wrote the word "proximity," we did not mean *immediate contact*; we merely wished to convey the idea, that we should remain in the country, where our brethren are in bonds, and *plead for them*, (which we could not do in Maryland) not leap over the wall, under the pretext of "shaping the policy of the American Continent."

But *we* too, have a question to ask. Our friend W., remarks that he has entertained the same opinions of the policy of emigration, from boyhood; aye, fifteen years ago, he was an emigrationist. "Did *you* mean what you wrote then?" If you did, how happens it that you are *here*, in 1853, still *talking loudly* about *leaving*? Why have *you* not been borne to the "tropical regions" by the current of "political events." We think we are at liberty to take your past history as a precedent for the future. "Time" will still continue, to "strengthen your convictions," but after all, you will settle down and resolve to *receive*, rather than impart that "reflex influence" which your imagination beholds so plainly, "removing the existing prejudice."

We believe with you, that Colonizationists would prefer that we should go to our "father land." We know they deprecate an independent community upon their "southern frontier." But they much more deprecate our existence in their midst. We are not disposed to compromise the matter with them, *by removing, but not removing* FAR.

But our friend concludes his letter by suddenly assuming a very hopeful mood. Well, better late than never. But his hope is *sui generis*. If he really hopes for our elevation here, why flee *from* the country? He declares that "those who would be free themselves, must strike the blow." But "did you mean what you wrote then?" If so, friend W., *you* must help *strike*, and not resolve to *receive* the blows and kicks of our enemies, and then depart in peace, for the tropical regions. But we must conclude, by calling upon our Emigration friends, to chase the evil spirit of despondency from their brow, and remember that "God is just, and his justice shall not sleep forever."

> "Ye fearful saints, fresh courage take,
> The clouds ye so much dread,
> Are big with mercy, and shall break,
> In blessings on your head."[38]

38. From William Cowper's "Light Shining out of Darkness," in his *Olney Hymns* (1779).

WHITFIELD'S SUR-REJOINDER[39]

Buffalo, N.Y., Dec. 30, 1853

MESSRS. EDITORS:—I have just got home, and read your comments upon my last letter, and must take upon myself to answer them as briefly as possible, even at the risk of being considered one of those individuals who "voluntarily, and cheerfully leap into the gladiatorial arena;" and that, not because I have any greater "proclivity to enter the arena of conflict," than you have, nor because I care much about personal misrepresentation; but because I protest against a great practical question, which I regard as vitally connected with our best interest, and which you seem to consider equally potent for evil-being misrepresented. In this connection, I desire to call your attention to your saying that I virtually accused you of dishonesty. Nothing could be farther from me than the intention to make any such charge. I trust that I have too much respect, both for you and myself, to make any such accusation. What I endeavored to expose was the unsoundness of your logic, not the dishonesty of your sentiments; and I think that your own article affords the evidence, that I succeeded in the attempt. To the question which *you* so triumphantly put, why, if I was an emigrationist fifteen years ago, I have not been borne to the tropical region by the current of political events? I would simply answer, that as I have never set myself up as a standard of rectitude, but on the contrary am conscious of numerous shortcomings, and faults of both omission and commission, I am content to plead guilty to the charge of not having acted up to my convictions of duty. Perhaps too, some extenuation may be found in the boy of sixteen, being more easily frightened from his course by the fierce attack of those whom he had been accustomed to revere as leaders and directors than the man of thirty. I have no doubt that I might have essentially bettered my condition

39. The "Sur-" suggests that Whitfield imagined this response being printed in *Frederick Douglass' Paper* above a response by Douglass or Watkins. There is no evidence that Douglass published the letter.

by emigrating fifteen years ago, but as united efforts are always better than isolated ones, my regret is much diminished by seeing the many good and true men who are now ready to enlist in this movement, to my future course, not being "a prophet, nor the son of a prophet,"[40] I shall not venture to contradict any prediction that you may see fit to make. It may be that I am as craven in spirit as you suppose, and that years of submission to oppression may so brutalize the mind as to render a menial position an acceptable one, but were such the case, I have yet to learn that it would be a good reason for remaining in such a position.

I perceive that my question has driven you from the false plea of proximity, to one of the real points at issue; which is, that you "do not believe in herding ourselves together in this country or any other"; you go on to state your own opinions, and the grounds on which we differ from you. While we recognize in you able and faithful ex-pounders of the doctrines of Anti-Emigrationists, we do not by any means acknowledge you as correct, or just interpreters of the principles which govern, or the influences which stimulate Emigrationists; and therefore respectfully ask to be allowed, also to present our views of the points at issue between us. Believing that we are better qualified to explain the principles which govern us, the measures we advocate and the motive which actuates us, than you can possibly be. You complain of the interminable prolixity of my letters. That fault might be in a great measure obviated if you would confine yourselves to the real points at issue, and argue against the measures and principles we really advocate, not undertake to make out a set of principles for us, and represent them as the ground we stand upon.

You devote a paragraph to what you are pleased to call the "egregious absurdity of this Cleveland Convention," because it does not propose to remove the whole nation. We see very frequently calls for National Conventions of the Liberty Party, and other parties, who

40. Amos 7:14.

constitute but a *very small* proportion of the nation, and while the callers of such conventions would be glad to see *all* the nation come up to their principles, they probably do not expect such a result. I pronounced the arguments upon an en masse emigration, pro. and con., to be unworthy a moment's consideration, not because I am opposed to en masse emigration, or would not labor earnestly for it if I thought that it could be accomplished, but my view of the laws which govern population, teach me that it is impossible, and it is foolish to talk of achieving impossibilities.

It is probable that the *very few* Puritans who emigrated to this country would hardly have come up to your idea of a nation, yet the lapse of two centuries, a very short period in national existence, has served to place them in quite a respectable position among the great nations of the earth.

Your question about the "uncongeniality of tropical climates, and the fatal folly of leaving a climate so congenial with our constitution, for one of sickness, devastation and death, or in other words the exchanging of a temperate for a torrid zone," might have some pertinence if I had ever made any such objections. My opinion on the comparative healthiness of the tropical and temperate climates, (and which I think could be proved conclusively were it not for the fear of subjecting myself to the charge of "interminable prolixity,") is that the diseases of tropical climates are far less numerous and complicated than those of temperate climates, and therefore so far from being the region "of sickness, devastation and death," the much-abused tropics are the most prolific seat of life, in both the animal and vegetable kingdom.

You represent Emigrationists as being "compounded with that despondency and despair which preclude the possibility of their working for their elevation here with that hopeful ardor which is the life-blood of the anti-slavery enterprise," and make the point of difference between us to be, that you "determined to remain here, battling for our rights; trusting in the willingness, and ability, and intention of Jehovah to crown your efforts with signal success." You also speak of being "an integrant part of this nation," from which you "will not willingly segregate yourselves." The real point of difference is not that we have any less faith in the willingness, ability, or intention of Jehovah to crown our efforts with success, but because we believe it to be a law of Jehovah, as fixed and immutable as Himself, that specific ends can be obtained only by the use of the adequate means.

Again you say neither Colonization, nor Emigration is a remedy for the ills of the colored American. He cannot emigrate from himself. He cannot destroy his own identity. If he leaves the country he must carry his tastes and predilections, with him. *If these are what they should be, he will here rise superior to the adverse circumstances by which he is surrounded. If they are not he will rise no where, but must ever occupy a degraded position.* If this means anything, it means that equal efforts put forth upon the part of the black men in this country, will raise them to an equal position with white men. An assumption which is most perniciously false, for nothing can be so well calculated to lead to the despair you so much deprecate as exciting false hopes, which must be disappointed. The only just reason to hope for the elevation of an oppressed class, is when they begin to examine the causes of their degradation in the fullest extent, to calculate what measures are necessary to promote their elevation, and then push them forward with all their might.

What then are the causes of the degradation of the black race in this country, and what the measures adequate to remove them? In every age of the world have been found classes of men oppressed by others, marked by some peculiarity of race, color, language, or religion, existing within a nation, but forming no "*integrant part*" of that nation; and "*segnated*," not by any act of their own, but by the inveterate hatred of the ruling class, from the rest of the community, as we are in the United States; and various has been their ultimate destiny. In some cases, where a country is invaded by a race of greater vigor and power, perpetual contests take place until the stronger party exterminates the weaker; as was the case with the Israelites in the land of Canaan, and the European colonists in this country. Where the oppressed class are sufficiently superior in numbers and physical strength, to make up for

the lack of intelligence and organization, they may succeed in revo-
lutionizing the country, and taking the government into their own
hands; as the blacks have done in Hayti. Or where the oppressed class
have the advantage of natural vigor, and superior numbers, but are
deficient in culture and development, they may go on steadily step
by step, improving their condition, until all the social and political
obstacles in their way are removed, and a complete fusion is effected,
leaving the stamp of the more numerous and vigorous race upon the
whole; as is the case with the present English race, in whose composi-
tion we find that the blood of the Norman master, has been forced to
give precedence to that of the Anglo-Saxon serf; and the same result
is being rapidly effected in South and Central America, by the absorp-
tion of all other races in the negro. But when the oppressed class are
but a small minority, scattered through the country, and the whole
organization of government is in the hands of their enemies, with all
its power wielded to crush them, as in the case of the French Hugue-
nots,[41] the British Puritans, and the American Negroes, Emigration
is the only resource. In such cases the whole mass never emigrate,
nor is it necessary that they should, (for there are always some who
have a hankering for the flesh-pots of Egypt, and had rather remain in
the service of those who despise them than encounter the privations
and hardships attendant upon building up a new country, and laying
broad and deep the foundations of a real national existence;) but it is
absolutely necessary as a preliminary to the elevation of a proscribed
class anywhere, that a portion of their number should go forth and
build up their own institutions, and conduct them in such a manner
as to furnish the ocular proof of their equal capacity, with the most
favored of mankind—to fulfill ably all the duties of the highest as
well as the lowest positions in society. Had it not been for the Puritan

41. Huguenots were Protestant reformers who were persecuted by French Catho-
lic authorities during the sixteenth and seventeenth centuries. In what became known
as the St. Bartholomew's Day Massacre, Catholics killed thousands of Huguenots in
Paris in October 1572.

emigration, and its effects upon the world, it is probable that religious toleration with many of the political reforms of Europe would not yet have been accomplished, and many who are now loud in their praises of the virtue and heroism of those emigrants, would still have been asking the question "can there be a church without a Bishop, or a State without a King." That question has been answered in such a manner as to frighten the Kings and Prelates of the old world, and make them tremble for the safety of their thrones. We must give a similar response to the question, is the negro capable of self-government?

In order for a people to act wisely and efficiently for the improvement of their condition, it becomes necessary to correctly understand that condition. The stronger the peculiar marks which distinguish the victims of oppressive laws from their oppressors, the stronger will be the prejudice and the harder to overcome it. Of all these differences color is the most obvious, for religion, language, manners and customs, may be changed, or assimilated, but "the Ethiopian cannot change his skin."[42] It is a natural consequence of the general freedom of this country, in religious and political matters, that slavery in order to sustain itself at all, must take a far more severe form than is necessary in any other country, and cast its victims entirely out of the pale of human sympathy. For while the Heathen, or the Mahommedan, may enfranchise, and fraternize all who embrace their creeds, and regard as the proper objects of slavery those infidels whom their religion teaches them, it is right to subdue and destroy; the evangelical Christians who profess to believe that God is no respecter of persons, that He has made of one blood all nations of men upon the face of the earth,[43] and has commanded them in all cases to do as they would be done by, finds no resource but in the hypothesis that the negroes are an inferior race, who find the highest development of which they are capable in a state of servitude to the whites; and, that therefore, slav-

42. Jeremiah 13:23.
43. Acts 17:26.

ery is a heaven ordained institution, established by God Himself, and sanctioned by Christ and His Apostles; and while the supporters of the monarchial and aristocratic governments of the old world, may readily advocate the extension to all the people of legal protection, and certain rights, which do not interfere with "the right divine of Kings to govern wrong,"[44] or the privileges of the higher orders, the American Democratic Republican, who professes to believe that all men are created equal, with the right to liberty and the pursuit to happiness, that taxation and representation should go together, that governments derive their just powers from the consent of the governed, and that equal suffrage is the only safeguard for political institutions, — can find as a political economist, no other excuse for slavery, and the fiendish legislation to which it has given rise, than that advanced by his brother theologian, that the negroes are an inferior race, who can aspire to no higher position than that of servile dependence upon the whites. Thus the American government, the American Churches, and the American people, are all engaged in one great conspiracy to crush us. Having adopted these as the fundamental grounds of the policy to be pursued with reference to the negro race, they endeavor to justify it, by trying to make the negro as brutal as they represent him to be. Hence, the utmost pains are taken to instill in him from childhood, a sense of his own inferiority; and any attempts on his part to rise above that position are resisted by the whole community.

Your assertion then, that if black men cannot rise here, they can rise no where, is utterly untrue, for in other countries he can have an equal chance with other men, which here he cannot have. Men of strong native genius, a Douglass, a Garnet, a Ward, a Crummell, a Pennington,[45]

---

44. From Alexander Pope's *The Dunciad* (1728–44), book 4, line 188.

45. The men named were prominent black abolitionist leaders: New Yorker Henry Highland Garnet (1815–82) rejected the moral suasion position of the Garrisonians and, at the 1843 National Convention of Colored Citizens in Buffalo, which Whitfield attended, delivered his famous speech, "An Address to the Slaves of the United States of America," presenting slave resistance as an act of patriotism and self-defense.

and such master spirits, may by the force of their own great intellects, raise themselves sufficiently high to show the world how great they might have become under more favorable circumstances. Such men are capable of rising under a pressure which would completely crush ordinary men. But do they reach the position that their talents, learning and character entitle them to occupy? By no means. But on the contrary, they are the first victims that this malignant prejudice selects to vent its spite upon. While the negro servant is allowed to pass with impunity, the negro editor is driven from the table, the negro clergyman dragged from the cars, the negro Doctor of Divinity spurned and abused on a common ferry boat. In short, while the negro *servant* is viewed with a certain degree of complacency, the negro *gentleman* is regarded with unmitigated hatred; and it is only when the negro attempts to improve himself, educate his family, and become a useful and respectable member of community, that he finds how inveterate is the prejudice which he must encounter. This prejudice meets him at every step, and contests with him every inch of ground, and acknowledges his equality only when he has proved his superiority; and it is idle to suppose that the negro can obtain full and fair equality in this country, until he can show at least an equality of attainments, and proportionate numbers occupying all the high positions in society. Could every colored man in the country be made a good mechanic,

He would eventually champion black emigration to Africa. Samuel Ringgold Ward (1817–ca. 1866), also of New York, founded two antislavery newspapers and authored *Autobiography of a Fugitive Negro* (1855). In 1851 he fled to Canada after his involvement with a fugitive slave case, and he emigrated to Jamaica in the late 1850s. Alexander Crummell (1819–98), an ordained Episcopal priest and leading antislavery figure in New York and Philadelphia, emigrated to Liberia in 1853 and remained there for twenty years. New York pastor J. W. C. Pennington (1807–70) wrote a pioneering volume of African American history, *A Textbook of the Origin and History of the Colored People* (1841), and was active in New York and British antislavery circles. In 1838 he performed the marriage between Frederick Douglass (under the name of Frederick Johnson) and Anna Murray shortly after Douglass escaped from slavery.

or placed in possession of a snug farm, it would not be sufficient to elevate him. They must have their full proportion of the professional men, legislators, jurists, authors, literati, merchants, mechanics, artists, capitalists, &c. With all the ordinary avenues of learning closed to us, and without the means of opening extraordinary ones, we must overcome all the obstacles in our path, until from our present state of ignorance, we shall equal the people who now claim to stand foremost in intellectual development, with greater facilities for progress than any other people have ever possessed; and with every lucrative employment closed to us, and we almost universally employed as their servants, we must become their equals in the proportionate number, and wealth of our capitalists, and business men, and even when all this is accomplished, equality does not follow. Wealth and intelligence, without political power and national organization, are not sufficient to raise a proscribed and degraded class to a full and fair equality. Witness the condition of the Jews throughout Christendom for more than a thousand years, and who, during all that period, were more wealthy than any other class, except perhaps the nobility, and more intelligent than any other class, except perhaps the clergy, and at the same time were more oppressed than any class whatever.

Having shown what attainments are necessary for our elevation here, let us see what are the prospects for obtaining them; and in this Frederick Douglass himself shall be our guide. In his letter to Mrs. Stowe he disposes of professional men, by stating that an educated people, which we do not possess, are necessary to sustain an educated ministry, and therefore pronounces an educated colored clergy a decided failure; and as white men will not employ colored lawyers to the evident detriment of their business, and as colored men cannot afford to suffer loss any more than the whites, black lawyers are as decided failures as the clergymen.[46] Another deficiency he finds, is that "slavery has robbed us of that self-reliance, so necessary to suc-

46. Douglass's letter to Harriet Beecher Stowe of 8 March 1853 was reprinted in the *Proceedings of the Colored National Convention*, 33–38.

cess;" and in order to increase our self-reliance, so that we may be able to compete successfully with the whites, he proposes to keep us here forever, under the immediate influence of that power which has destroyed all our self-respect. At last he comes to the well established fact, that colored men by the pressure of European emigration, are fast being deprived of the menial employments of which they formerly enjoyed the monopoly, and he proposes to remedy it by making them generally mechanics, a class whom he admits regard us with a more invincible prejudice than any other, and to that prejudice add the selfish fear of being deprived of their own employments. By what kind of reasoning he expects us to succeed in the higher employments, when the prejudice is so invincible, while pressure of circumstances is fast driving us from the menial occupations, where alone we are tolerated with any degree of complacency, I am at a loss to know; especially, when according to *his* description of us, from our "lack of self respect, and want of enterprise," we would be totally unfitted to succeed in the former, but peculiarly adapted to the latter, or menial class of employments.

Your quotation from the Broadway Tabernacle speech of Frederick Douglass might be received as good emigration doctrine, with the exception of the two last sentences, which recommend a course of "masterly inactivity" to the blacks of this country, and express "faith in the wisdom and *justice*" of the whites. I believe with him that "the fact that these twelve millions of people (and if we take the rule which prevails in this country, and turn all who have any taint to the negro, we may add eight or nine millions more) are tending to the one point upon this continent, is not without signification, but clearly indicate that a home, a country, a nationality, are all attainable this side of Liberia." But, unlike him, I have NO faith left in the *justice* of this country and believing that God helps those who help themselves, I shall do what little lies in my power towards promoting a *real* national organization.

Emigrationists are not as you assert, "confounded with despondency and despair." On the contrary, no class of men are fired with more hopeful ardor, and that not because we look for any miraculous interposition from Jehovah in our behalf, but because we believe we are acting in accordance with His immutable laws, by adopting the measures which our judgment shows us is necessary for the elevation of our race. You say that I "must help strike, not receive the blows and kicks of our enemies," et cetera. That is very good advice, and what I am now striving to follow. The man whose limbs are pinioned may writhe and twist in his chains, but his efforts will be fruitless. If he is wise he will first free himself from the manacles, and then take a position where his blows will tell upon the head of the enemy. I shall endeavor to place myself where I *can help* strike an effective blow against the common foe; not turn round and lick the dirt from the foot that kicks me, express my "faith in the wisdom and *justice*" of the men who trample me under their feet, and declare that I "will not *segregate*" myself from those who spurn me from their path. Neither shall I follow the course so generally pursued by our people in their conventions, prating about this as the land of their birth, and claiming with all its faults to love it still; as our brethren of Illinois in their late State Convention, after enumerating certain enactments which for malignant cruelty, pitiful meanness, and shameful profligacy, surpass any laws ever enacted upon the face of the earth, and might make the most malignant fiend of hell recoil with horror at their unparalleled atrocity, call the power that enacts such laws "our glorious and well-beloved State," and express confidence in its *justice*, and *generosity*. Dr. Johnson defined patriotism to be the last refuge of a scoundrel.[47] But a *black patriot* in this country must be more fool than knave. The fact is, I have no country, neither have you, and your assumption that you are an *integrant* part of *this* nation, is not true. The ruling class, whatever you may say, do not, and *will* not, regard you as forming any "integrant part of this nation." You may declare that you will not "segregate" yourselves from them, and you will not "herd with" your

47. In his *Life of Samuel Johnson* (1791), Boswell reports that Johnson made this pronouncement the evening of 7 April 1775.

own people, but they will teach you that you cannot herd with them, except upon the terms that a servant herds with his master. You may resolve "to plant your trees in American soil, and quietly repose in the shade thereof;" but that *repose* will be neither sweet, nor refreshing.

Black men should labor not to excite pity, but to command respect. They can never be acknowledged as the equals of their oppressors, until they attain an equal position, pecuniarily, intellectually, morally and politically. I believe that the negro race are sufficiently superior in natural vigor of mind and body, to overcome the present differences, and attain that equality, if they can be placed in circumstances which will allow the full development of their powers; and I think sufficient evidence of that superiority is given in the fact, that in spite of the unparalleled obstacles in the way of their improvement, they are progressing faster than any other class in this land of progress; and are constantly diminishing the distance between them and their oppressors. But I do not believe that they are so much superior to all other men, as to be able to overcome a concatenation of obstacles, such as were never presented to any class of men before, without using the proper means. It is therefore, their duty to get out of a situation where all the profits of their labor go to strengthen their oppressors, and rivet the chain upon themselves; and take a position where their labors will help to improve and elevate their race. With the highest respect, I remain yours, in favor of independent policy.

J. M. WHITFIELD

APPENDIX

CANADA WEST

Climate.—Salubrious. Winters, though long and cold, are more moderate than in the greater parts of Maine, New Hampshire and Vermont, in consequence of being partly in more Southern latitudes and farther westerward.

Soil.—Black and sandy loam. Clay and sand; the black loam predominates.

Timber.—Walnut, hickory, white and burr oak, basswood, ash, pine and poplar of the largest size.

Grains and Vegetables.—Wheat, buckwheat, rye, oats, barley, potatoes, cucumbers, onions, beans, cabbage, beets, egg plants, peas, leeks, celery, lettuce, asparagus, melons, cantelopes and spinage.

Meats.—Beef, mutton, veal and pork.

Price of Lands.—Government lands from 37½ cts. to $4.00 per acre. Private sales from $3 to $100 per acre.

Political Rights.—All are equal in the eye of the law.

Population.—Consist of English, Scotch, Irish, French, white and colored emigrants from the U.S., and numbers in the western province about one million, 35,000 of whom are colored.

Colored Settlements.—Dawn, Buxton, Wilberforce, and the Refugees' Home.

Remarks.—"Canada West, is emphatically the only refuge where the colored American can enjoy liberty and equality, this side of the Gulf of Mexico." H. BIBB.

"The conclusion arrived at in respect to Canada, by an impartial person, is, that no settled country in America offers stronger inducements to colored people." MARY A. SHADD.[48]

48. Mary Ann Shadd Cary (1823–93), a free black from Delaware, taught at African American schools before emigrating to Canada West in 1851. There she emerged as an influential editor of the Canadian black journal the *Provincial Freeman.*

JAMAICA

Climate.—One of the most pleasant and delightful in the world.

Extent.—150 miles long; average breadth, 50 miles.

Population.—380,000, of which number, 364,000 are colored, and 16,000 whites.

Condition of the Colored Inhabitants.—A considerable number of the principal gentlemen of the Island are colored. The House of Assembly is composed in part of colored gentlemen. A large part of the lawyers, physicians, leading merchants and wealthy men are also colored. Most every man possesses a freehold, and is therefore, entitled to vote at the elections for their own rulers.

Improvements.—The country is intersected by roads, the streams crossed by bridges, and cultivation extends even to the very summits of the mountains.

Chance for Emigrants.—Large tracts of level open land can be obtained at a comparatively low price, and there is abundant employment for laborers, mechanics, and those who wish to settle down as farmers.

Productions.—Indian and Guinea corn, wheat, oats, sweet potatoes, peas, beans, turnips, carrots, sugar, coffee, chocolate yams, bananas, figs, grapes, arrow roots, ginger, tapioca, vegetable oils, ground nuts, cotton, tobacco, cinnamon, cloves, pine apples, oranges, lemons, &c.

Face of the Country.—A range of mountains traverse the whole length of the Island, which are intersected by the purest streams of water, that irrigates the plains and the valleys.

Soil.—Remarkably fertile; a day and a half's labor in each week of the most indifferent cultivation, will produce a year's support.

Prices of Produce.—About three times as much remuneration is given to the producer for his articles, as are given in the States. For instance: Corn per bushel, $1,25 cts., milk, 12½ cts. a quart.

Remarks.—"I do not know that there is any other country, which could offer you [the colored people] the same advantages. [As

Jamaica.][49] Canada, I know, does not. It is a cold country, with a most severe winter; there the great bulk of the population is composed of different races, and it is destined to be peopled with Europeans. But the great advantage which Jamaica has over it, is, that it is essentially a colored country. There the whites are a mere handful, and instead of being at variance with the colored people, they are on the most amicable terms with them." WM. WEMYSS ANDERSON.[50]

"Jamaica is emphatically, my next choice after Canada. Should I be ever tempted to leave Western Canada, it shall be to repose under my own 'vine and fig tree,' in that delightful Island, which can be done there in the most literal sense of that term. To all of our people who intend to migrate southward, my advice is, by all means go to Jamaica." H. BIBB.

HAYTI

Description. — The same description of soil, climate, productions, &c., that is given above of Jamaica, may be applied to this country.

Remarks. — "This Empire, as is well known, is wholly in the hands of colored men, and forms the grandest centre of attraction for our race wheresoever scattered around the globe. It is the first nationality established by our race, sacred through the means of revolution against tyrannical oppression. It was the second independent government established in America. And that independence has been creditably maintained ever since, under the most adverse circumstances, and that too by a people just emerged from slavery, and wholly unacquainted with the arts of political administration. In 1824 President Boyer[51] of-

49. The parentheticals are Newsom's.

50. From William Wemyss Anderson's *A Description and History of the Island of Jamaica* (1851).

51. Jean-Pierre Boyer (1778–1850) was president of Haiti from 1818 to 1843. In 1824 he invited African Americans to settle in Haiti, offering land grants and travel expenses.

fered great inducements to the colored Americans to settle in that country, and several thousands did go from the U.S. But it is a matter of surprise that this emigration entirely ceased after a few years duration, and a knowledge of the existence of such a country has become almost entirely obscured. Every colored man should feel binding upon himself the duty to sustain the national existence of Hayti, intact against the intervention of any or all powers whatsoever, and should pursue a policy to that end. Emigration there in large numbers on the part of the colored Americans would do much to strengthen the hands of that government, and forward in an uncalculable degree the cause of our elevation in America. From that point we could watch the fate of our brethren in Cuba, and prepare ourselves to lend them a helping hand, when the day of their reckoning shall come."[52]

Principal Towns and Seaports.—Port au Prince, Aux Cayes, Haytieu, Jacmel, Jeremie and Gonaives, that carry on an extensive commercial business with the United States, Great Britain, France and other maritime powers, by the export of mahogany, logwood, coffee, coca, &c; and the import of flour, pork, beef, articles of manufacture, &c. All of these ports are within 10 to 14 days sail of Boston, New York, and Philadelphia, and the fare in vessels from these places out there, are from $15 to $50.   J. T. HOLLY.

CENTRAL AMERICA

Description.—The productions of the last two places, may, with a little variation be applied to this country.

Principal points for Emigration.—The British Settlement, and the Mosquito Kingdom.

The British Settlement is situated on the Bay of Honduras, between

---

52. This paragraph was in all likelihood written by James T. Holly, who would publish his major work on Haiti, *Vindication of the Capacity of the Negro Race*, in 1857.

15 deg. 30 min., and 19 deg. 30 min., north latitude. Balize, principal town and seaport; population, 6000, of which 4000 are colored, who are principally engaged in cutting, sawing, and exporting mahogany. The Mosquito Kingdom is situated between 11 and 15 deg., north latitude, on the Mosquito Gulf. This is an Independent Kingdom of Indians and negroes, under the protection of Great Britain. It is the key to a country that possesses great natural resources and commercial advantages awaiting the hand of enterprising industry to develop them to an almost illimitable extent.

Remarks.—"Our best policy is to migrate immediately to Central America, intercept the farther progress of the Anglo-American southward, and prepare to inaugurate a new era in the world, by developing the colored races on the southern portions of the continent to a higher degree of christianity and civilization than the world has ever yet introduced." REV. WM. C. MUNROE.

SOUTH AMERICA

Principal Points.—Guiana and Columbia.

Description of Guiana.—Lies between 80 deg. 40 min. north latitude, and 3 deg. 30 min. south latitude, and the 50th and 60th degrees of longitude west of Greenwich. Greatest length 1,090 geographical miles; greatest breadth 710 geographical miles.

How Divided.—Into Brazilian, French, Dutch, British, and Venezualian Guiana. The most important of which, is British Guiana.

Population of British Guiana.—100,000.

Staple Products.—Sugar, rum, and coffee.

Principal Town.—Georgetown—in the country of Demerara, British Guiana,—contains a population of 24,000. Streets wide, traversed with canals; the houses generally surrounded by a garden, or large trees.

Description of Columbia.—Columbia occupies an extent of 22 deg., or 1,320 miles of longitude, and 18 deg., or 1,080 miles of latitude, extending from 6 deg. 30 min. south, to 11 deg. 30 min. north of the equator. It is divided into the States of New Grenada and Venezuela.

Productions. — At the height of 4,000 feet above the level of the sea, vegetation continues uninterrupted throughout the year, and wheat, leguminous plants, and all the productions of the temperate zones are produced abundantly. On the plains, sugar, cotton, coffee, cocoa, indigo, tobacco, and every species of tropical productions.

Population. — About 4000,000; composed of Indians, Spaniards, Creoles, Africans, and the mixed blood of Mulattoes, Mestisoes, Quarterous, &c.

Remarks— "In British Guiana, there is an extent of territory which it is said, will sustain a population of one hundred millions. That fine country I hold to be one of the homes of the colored population; and whoever possesses it as an heritage, will possess the key to South America, both east and west, if they be an industrious, intelligent, and free people. Look well to these things; ponder them in your hearts; talk of them by your firesides, and by the wayside; and prepare yourselves for a great future. Let me repeat, that it is my firm conviction that God intends to build you up a mighty people on these continents, and that He will compensate you and your children for all the tears you have shed in your afflictions, the flood that has been spilt by your oppressors, and the toils you have been compelled to endure for others." *Address of John Scoble to the Colored People.*[53]

---

53. The British abolitionist John Scoble (1799–ca. 1867) worked to arouse British opposition to slavery in the southern Americas, publishing *British Guiana* in 1837 (his "Address" was probably delivered around the same time). He founded the British and Foreign Anti-Slavery Society in 1839 and served as its secretary from 1842 to 1852.

NOTE

If the present edition of this *Pamphlet*, meets with a general public favor and patronage; and the wants of our people for more general information, is manifested, by an early disposal of it, we propose to publish another edition, with an enlarged Appendix, containing the politics, commercial resources, advantages of the countries referred to in the foregoing Appendix, and the facilities for emigrants from the United States, to engage in the pleasant and independent, as well as lucrative business of husbandry.   w. t. newsom.

FROM THE VISION[54]

CANTO SECOND

OH! Superstition! sovereign dame,
We praise and bless thy glorious name,
Who from thy all prolific womb,
   Us, thy true children, did'st bring forth,
To spread a dark and fearful gloom
   O'er the inhabitants of earth.
'Neath my broad flag each deadly crime
   Engendered in the depths of hell,
Shall travel on from clime to clime,
   The tide of human woe to swell.
In every region of the earth,
   Wherever lives a human soul,
My myrmidons[55] shall sally forth,
   And bind it under thy control,
Stir in each breast a deadly ire,
Kindle a fierce, devouring fire
Of bitter discord, hate and strife,
Appeased by naught but human life;
And all the highest blessings given
   To purify the soul of man,
And fit it for the joys of heaven,
   Through us shall prove his direst ban;
Even the sexual love bestowed
   As means to propagate his race,

54. Whitfield published Canto Second of "The Vision" over three issues of *Frederick Douglass' Paper*: 24 June, 1 July, and 8 July 1853. Canto First probably appeared in issues that are no longer extant, lost in the fire at Douglass's Rochester home in 1872. The evidence suggests that the poem consists of two cantos (see nn. 58 and 60).

55. Loyal followers or subordinates, with sources in the legendary Thessalian people who followed their king Achilles into the Trojan War.

From its high purposes shall be bowed
    To consummate his deep disgrace;
And burning lust, and lewd desire,
Kindling a foul, unhallowed fire,
Shall then usurp the place and name
Of pure affection's holy flame.
Where pure connubial love should dwell
    In heaven's brightest livery dressed,
The foulest passions known in hell
    Shall agitate the tortured breast.
By dark intrigue, and secret vile,
    We'll scatter in the minds of men,
Such lessons of deceit and guile,
    That fiends shall stand astonished, when
They see the scenes of war and woe
Which from those dark deceptions flow.
Throughout the devastated earth
Shall spread such scenes of hellish birth,
That honesty, and sterling worth,
Known only as fit themes for mirth,
Shall swell in woe and want obscure,
    While round them flaunt on every side,
In rank, and pomp, and wealth secure,
    The pampered slaves of lust and pride.
Around the fair domestic hearth
    Where pure, fraternal love should rest,
Where sportive glee and joyous mirth,
    Should find a home in every breast;
The poisonous seed which we will sow
    With every hostile feeling rife,
Shall round those household altars throw
    The shades of discord, hate and strife.
The brother by the brother's arm
    Slaughtered in deadly feud shall fall,

While all around the rude alarm
  Shall turn fraternal love to gall.[56]
The father armed against the son,
  The son against the sire shall rise,
And we'll rejoice, as one by one,
  They fall a welcome sacrifice
Upon thy blood-stained altar stone—
For there each wail and heart-wrung groan,
Shall sound to thy approving ears
Sweet as the music of the spheres,
With rank, and pomp, and gold, and gems,
With laurel wreaths and diadems,
We'll deck the warrior's blood-stained brow
And make the trampled people bow
In humble homage to his state.
Supported by their blood and sweat;
And he whose devastating hand
Spreads deadliest slaughter through the land,
Whose only right to rank and fame
Are mighty cities wrapt in flame,
Whose claims to be considered good
Are laurels drenched in human blood,
Whose title to the name of wise
Lies in the monstrous sacrifice
Of human life and happiness,
  And every good that sweetens life,
The spread of woe and wretchedness,
  Of want and misery, hate and strife—
Shall be the one on whom the crowd
Will heap applauses long and loud,
And cause the truly good and great,
Who sought great evils to abate,

56. Bile; rancor.

Who labored to reform the State,
And by pure teachings to create
A love of virtue, truth and right,
   A hatred of the false and wrong,
Which should protect the weak-one's right,
   And check the encroachments of the strong—
To yield the place of power and fame
   To him whose only aim through life
Has been to gain a mighty name
   By sacrifice of human life.
Regardless of the want and woe
Which must from such contention flow;
And thus make wisdom, virtue, right,
Give place to lawless power and might.
With false ideas of honor's laws
   We'll lead the minds of men astray,
Till for each slight and trivial cause
   They seek their dearest friends to slay,
And claim, to justify the feud,
The sanction of that bloody code,
Which desecrates bright honor's name
By ruthless deeds of blood and shame.
We'll kindle in the monarch's heart
   Ambition's fierce and baleful fire,
And lead him on to play the part
   Which all our interest require;
We'll set before his dazzled eye
   Visions of glory, power and fame,
And as they pass in grandeur by
   His soul shall kindle with the flame;
And spread throughout each neighboring land
The tide of battle, blood and brand.
We'll plant within the Bigot's mind
   Such overweening pride and zeal,

That with religious frenzy blind,
   He'll seek to spread by fire and steel
O'er all the earth his own vile faith,
And glory in the scenes of death
Which from the persecutions rise,
Exulting in the sacrifice
Of human life that meets his eye,
Smile to see unbelievers die,
Nor care how many victims bleed,
So the harsh tenets of his creed
Are made to spread throughout the earth,
And fetter from their very birth
The minds of men, and thus secure
The eternal thraldom of the poor,
Thus training from their very birth
   The people for tyrannic rule,
Enabling priest throughout the earth
   To make the human race their tool,
With which to build up gorgeous fanes,[57]
   Where costly pomp, and sacrifice,
Mingled with rich, harmonious strains,
   Shall rise as incense to the skies,
And draw from heaven a withering blight
   Upon the impious heads of those
Who practice such blasphemous rite
   Built upon human wrongs and woes,
And offer up to mercy's God,
As sacrifice, their brother's blood.
The heartless Demagogue we'll find,
   And clothe his tongue with specious lies,
That he may lead the people blind—

57. Temples.

And while before their dazzled eyes
He seems to play the patriot's part,
We'll sow corruption in his heart;
And while the rabble tune their lays,
And sing loud paeans in his praise,
And real patriots retire
   Disgusted from the senseless show,
And moan to see the holy fire
   Of liberty reduced so low,
That sycophants and parasites,
   May prostitute the glorious name,
And use the reverence it excites
   To cover up the deeds of shame;
We'll blind the people's eyes, that they
May fall a sure and easy prey
Into the treacherous hands of those
Who prove their country's direst foes,
By placing lawless power and might
In place of virtue, truth and right.[58]

We'll plant within the ruler's mind
   Such maxims of despotic power,
That to all liberal movements blind,
   Swayed by the impulse of the hour;
They'll fight against each wise reform
   The people's interest require,
And thus increase the gathering storm
   Ere long to burst in clouds of fire,
Spreading wild anarchy abroad,
And smiting with unsparing rod,

58. This ends the section of "The Vision" published in the 24 June 1853 issue of *Frederick Douglass' Paper*, p. 4.

The high and low, the bad and good,
In one wild scene of war and blood.
Thus skillfully by turns we'll bring,
    The Anarch and the Tyrant forth,
The Demagogue and despot King,
    To spread destruction through the earth:
As, alternately each bears sway,
And marks the people for his prey,
We'll sow dissensions in the crowd,
Till murmurs rise to clamors loud,
Till despotism shorn of power
Before rebellion's hosts shall cower,
While revolution sweeps along
    With wildest horrors in its train,
We'll stir the passions of the throng;
    And while true patriots strive in vain
To supersede the despot's might
By reign of order, law and right,
To ravage, desolate and kill,
    We'll raise unto the highest top,
The meanest of the dregs that fill
    The cup of human vileness up.
Here ruthless rapine bearing sway,
There bloody broils and mortal fray,
The common order of the day;
Till gloomy horror seizes all,
And in their apathy they fall,
Obedient to the despot's call;
And in his power seek to find
Rest from that frenzy, fierce and blind,
Which, in bright Freedom's holy name,
Can perpetrate the grossest shame,
And make the tyrant's arm more strong
To consummate his deeds of wrong.

Thus will we bring each wild extreme,
   Successively to bear the rule,
Till real liberty shall seem
An idle visionary dream,
   Vain, as the babblings of a fool;
And all who make its praise their theme,
Or seek to throw a single gleam
   Of its pure light, upon the den,
Where foul corruption weaves its scheme
   To hold in thrall the minds of men;
Fiercely assailed on every side,
By minions of tyrannic pride,
And by the false and fickle throng,
Who blend all sense of right and wrong
In vainly striving to redress
Their wrongs by riot and excess,
All unregarded shall remain,
Their prudent counsel urged in vain,
While o'er their heads to bear the rule
They see advanced the knave or fool.
Thus misery, and want, and woe,
Throughout the earth shall ceaseless flow,
Till all are brought to humbly bow,
And at thy altar pay their vow.
Then, meanly cringing in the dust,
Recreant to every sacred trust,
They shall receive with servile awe
Thy mandates as their highest law;
While we triumphant at thy side,
Throughout the earth will proudly ride,
Exulting in the sacrifice,
Which from thy blood-stained altars rise.
Soon as he ceased, from all the crowd
Burst forth applauses long and loud,

While through their bristling ranks there ran
   A feeling of ecstatic joy
That soon upon the race of man
   They'd fall to ravage and destroy.
Then Slavery with a jet black flag,
   Advanced, and thus in lofty tone,
Bowing, addressed the hideous hag
   Who sat exalted on the throne;
Not War and his fierce train alone
Shall be supporters of thy throne,
And seek by every means to bind
Thy chains upon the human mind,
And make perforce each struggling soul
Acknowledge thy supreme control;
For we will bring our powerful aid
   To help sustain thy tottering throne,
And many a soul by us betrayed
   Shall utter forth the heart-wrung groan,
And mourning wail, and bitter cries,
   Which make sweet music to thy ear,
And thou'lt accept the sacrifice,
   While we with purpose most sincere,
Strive for to spread thy power abroad
Till men shall know no other God—
Seek to obey no higher power,
And to thy dark dominion cower.
To execute thy stern decrees,
And thy fierce nature to appease,
Weave in with each religious creed
The sanction of some guilty deed;
With every form and mode of faith,
Incorporate the seeds of death,
Till every earthly fane shall be,
Whate'er its creed or faith may be,

A temple for to worship thee,
In all thy dark iniquity.
When men grow tired of deadly feud,
And seek respite from deeds of blood,
Be it my care that nothing good
In lieu thereof shall e'er intrude.
Though men may sate their vengeful ire,
    And for a time lay war aside,
Of our foul deeds they'll never tire,
    We'll pamper so their lust and pride.
'Neath my black flag each noxious vice
    Shall flourish and grow proud and strong,
While many a cunning, false device
    Shall so confound the right and wrong,
That men, unable to discern
    The principles of truth and right,
Shall yield to Slavery's mandate stern,
    And bow to lawless power and might.
Gross ignorance throughout the earth
    Shall spread abroad its sable pall,
And thus shall fetter from their birth
    In darkest gloom the minds of all.
The priest the fetters of his creed,
    Shall throw around the youthful mind,
Till ripe for any bloody deed,
    To reason deaf—to nature blind,
They cringe with superstitious awe,
    Acknowledging no higher power,
Receive his dogmas as their law,
    And 'neath his maranathas[59] cower;
And thus become the fitting tool
    To spread by dark and bloody deeds,

59. Invocations to God; see 1 Corinthians 16:22.

Over the earth the priestly rule,
   Which binds them to their own false creeds.
The priesthood, too, we'll glaze and blind,
And stir up every honest mind
With such enthusiastic zeal,
That, laboring for the Church's weal,
They care not what the means may be,
Nor seek to know what tyranny
Is used, so numerous proselytes
Conform to their religious rites.
Thus will we bend the human mind
   In servile fear to priestly sway,
Then set the blind to lead the blind,
   Till all the race are led astray,
Till priest and people all are lost
   In the dark maze of doubtful creeds
And find unto their bitter cost
   That true religion lies in deeds,
And not in creeds and formal rites,
   In hollow vows and empty faith
Or furious zeal, which takes delight
   In every unbeliever's death.
When men grow tired of War's wild reign,
   And thy dark altars reek no more
With the sweet savors of the slain,
   Who fell 'mid battle's awful roar;
Be it mine to see that to thy throne
Shall still ascend the dying groan,
The mourning wail and bitter cries,
The scalding tear, and swelling sighs,
Which round thee like sweet incense rise,
And make accepted sacrifice.
For though the warrior's hand may spare
   The foe he seized in war's wild fray,

A darker fate will we prepare
   For those who 'scape the battle day.
Bound in oppression's iron chain,
Consigned to anguish, woe and pain,
They shall regret they were not slain
With others on the battle plain,
And spared the harrowing sight to see
The life of woe and misery,
Of galling chains and slavery,
Awaiting their posterity.
Thus we will so arrange our plan
That the whole family of man
Bound down by slavery's blighting chain,
To latest ages shall remain
Buried in superstitious night,
Chained down by form, and creed, and right,
Shall never hear of Freedom bright,
Or see religion's holy light.
The master we will draw aside
And fill his heart with lust and pride.
Till swelling with unbounded power,
He makes his vassals cringe and cower
Beneath his passion's fierce display,
And, ruling with unbounded sway,
Shall smite weak youth and hoary age,
As victims of his fiendish age;
And all the keenest tortures wield
To make his female victims yield
Their persons to his brutal lust,
And o'er such ruthless scenes accursed,
Where many a noble, brilliant mind
   That might on learning's brightest page,
   Have lighted up and led his age,
To darkest ignorance consigned;

Bound to some stupid ruffian's will,
Forever doomed his fields to till—
To tremble at his brutal frown,
   Or fawn and cringe beneath his smile,
Each manly impulse trodden down
   By false deceit, or cunning wile,
Finds out that for the wretched slave
   No rest is known but in the grave.[60]

Where virgin purity betrayed
Appeals to heaven in vain for aid,
And female chastity is made
A staple article of trade,
The pampered priests who claim to be
   The consecrated ones of heaven,
Look on those scenes complacently,
   And then pronounce the sins forgiven,
Of men who their own children sell,
   Wretches so steeped in vice and shame
That all the fiends from heaven that fell,
   And expiate in endless flame,
Their guilt may from hell's dungeons peep,
   And in such scenes exulting see
That there is still a lower deep
   Of shame, if not of misery;
A lower deep, a fiercer flame,
For those who in religion's name

60. This ends the section of "The Vision" published in the 1 July 1853 issue of *Frederick Douglass' Paper*, p. 4. At the end of the section, Douglass printed "CONCLUDED NEXT WEEK." The concluding section that follows was printed in the 8 July 1853 issue of *Frederick Douglass' Paper*, p. 4, and was titled "The Vision: Canto Second.—Concluded."

Rear temples to the living God,
Built with the price of human blood.
Thus every foul, degrading vice,
    Which lurks within the human mind,
We'll bring by calculations nice,
By many a subtle, false device,
    To spread destruction, fierce and blind,
    O'er the whole race of human kind;
And every manly attribute
    In full subjection basely bind,
And to the level of the brute
    Debase the noblest powers of mind.
In every region of the earth
    Where my foul followers bear the sway,
    And claim the people for their prey,
The darkest scenes of hellish birth,
Of gloom and horror shall spread forth,
    With every returning day;
New scenes of terror and affright,
Return with each returning night,
Intemperance, bearing in its train,
The liquid fire that sears the brain,
Shall blast with foul pestiferous breath
    Each goodly object in his path,
Spread misery, disease and death,
    Rouse burning hate and frenzied wrath,
Till every region shall be rife
With deeds of shame and deadly strife
And shameless lust shall boldly lead
    The revels of its numerous crew,
And urge by many a loathsome deed,
    Their brutal midnight orgies through,
While jarring strife and noisy brawl,
Spreads wild confusion over all.

From many a foul and loathsome haunt
  Of low debauchery, gross and vile,
Shall wanton harlots gaily flaunt,
  And draw by many an artful wile
The unsuspecting to their snare,
And strive to drown their own despair,
By draining deep the deadly bowl,
Whose poisonous contents fire the soul,
Inflame the blood and craze the brain,
And bring forth all the ghastly train
Of dire diseases, pain and woe,
Which must inevitably flow
From Nature's violated law,
And heavy retribution draw
Upon the impious heads of those
Who their Creator's laws oppose,
Their noblest attributes deprave,
And every faculty enslave;
And thus progress from bad to worse,
Exposed unto that dreadful curse,
Which throws around transgression's path
Offended Heaven's blasting wrath.
Full many a deed of loathsome name
  Shall desolate the ravaged earth,
While millions, writhing in their shame,
  Shall curse the hour that gave them birth;
And in their frenzy strive to drown
The still small voice of conscience down,
Indulge in many a vile excess,
Its silent workings to redress;
Till vice untrammeled bears the sway,
And artless virtue falls a prey,
And each vile passion shall go forth
Reigning triumphant through the earth.

Hence Lust, with foul lascivious eye,
Shall seize on virgin purity,
Deceit shall mire beneath deceit,
The Liar shall the Liar cheat,
Traitor to Traitor false shall prove,
And hate shall every bosom move;
Here swelling pride shall seek to make
   His fellows tremble at his nod,
At his imperious mandate quake
   As though they heard the voice of God,
While avarice in eager mood
   Shall gloat o'er his ill-gotten gain,
Not caring though a brother's blood
   The heaps of glittering gold may stain;
The drunkard shall rejoice to see
   His brother drunkard's beastly fall,
Thus will we plant fierce enmity
   And bring destruction on them all.
Then, ruling with unbounded sway,
While death and misery mark their way,
Shall vice and crime forever reign,
Exulting in the woe and pain
Which strews their desolated path
With trophies of vindictive wrath.
And every torturing pang that wrings
   The breasts of devils damned in hell,
Shall bring its keen, envenomed stings,
   To pierce the hearts of those who dwell
In careful safety on the earth,
And change there scenes of joyous mirth,
To writhing pain and bitter woe,
While, dealing with an unseen foe,
They mark their brightest prospects fall,
And disappointment cover all.

While we, exulting in their shame,
Sing paeans to thy mighty name,
And as we bind the galling chain
The source of all their woe and pain,
And force them all to bend the knee,
And humble homage pay to thee,
Demons shall join the loud acclaim,
     And as they help the sound to swell,
     Shall make the lowest depths of hell
Resound with praises of thy name;
Till earth and hell in concert join,
To worship at thy horrid shrine.
Through every land, in every tongue,
     Shall prayer and incense rise to thee,
And loftiest hymns of praise be sung
     To thee as their chief Deity.
Millions shall rise with wild acclaim,
And sing loud anthems to thy name;
Thus vice, and crime, and shame, and woe,
Throughout the earth shall ceaseless flow,
And we, thy ministers, will spread
Fierce vengeance on each rebel head,
Who dares thy mandates to oppose,
Or rank itself among thy foes.
He ceased, and one terrific yell
     From those assembled bands burst forth,
While echo through the caves of hell,
     And farthest regions of the earth,
Conveyed the wild, exultant cry,
Which told to all beneath the sky,
That Earth and all her sons should be
A prey to War and Slavery.
That Superstition's withering blight
     Shall spread its deepening gloom around,

Till buried in the darkest night,
   The human race shall all be found
By stupid faith in senseless creeds,
To perpetrate such guilty deeds,
That Superstition shall go forth
With War and Slavery through the earth,
Reigning with full, unbounded sway
Till all the people fall a prey.
Till shameless vice and hardened crime
   Make honesty and virtue flee,
And wrap Religion's truths sublime,
   To sanction War and Slavery;
Upon the throne of mercy's God,
Erect their idols stained with blood,
And from his pure and holy law
Their creeds of hate and vengeance draw.
Soon as the clamor of their cries
Had ceased to echo through the skies,
The Gorgon[61] rising from her throne
Upon those hosts looked proudly down,
And thus addressed the mighty pair
   Who o'er the rest as leaders stood,
The black and scarlet flags to bear
   Through scenes of darkness, crime, and blood.
Well have ye spoke, my children true,
   Promised my power to sustain,
When deeds of darkness are to do,
   And help to spread my reign.
Now o'er the earth we'll wing our flight,

---

61. In Greek mythology, a monstrous female creature who turns all who look at her into stone.

And while the gloomy shades of night
Settle upon the human mind,
And leave the race in darkness blind,
By many a foul and loathsome blight,
We'll quench each ray of dawning light,
Till Superstition reigns alone,
And War and Slavery prop their throne.
Then with one wild exultant cry
That seemed to rend[62] the vaulted sky,
And make the yawning caves of hell
Re-echo to the fiendish yell,
They took their flight o'er land and sea
To work their dark iniquity.
Quicker than flies a ray of light
Each form had vanished from the sight,
And as I stood in wonder there,
The scene melted into air—
Mountain and lake, and throne were gone,
And I in silence stood alone.

MORNING SONG[63]

AWAKE! 'tis morn,
    The brilliant dawn
Has ushered in the day;
    The Queen of night
    Has paled her light,
The morning star its ray.

---

62. Douglass's compositor has "mend" here, but "rend" seems more likely.
63. From *Frederick Douglass' Paper*, 28 July 1854, 4.

Arise, and hark!
The warbling lark
Pours forth its morning lay,
And seems to praise
The sun's bright rays
Which gild the opening day.

Each bud and flower,
From field and bower,
Sheds fragrance all around!
While through the trees
The murmuring breeze
Whispers with gentle sound.

While notes of praise
In varied lays
From all the earth arise,
Pour forth thy song
In notes more strong
And let it reach the skies.

And bear above
Such strains of love
As none but thou canst raise,
Save angel choirs
Who tune their lyres
To sing Jehovah's praise.

REPORT ON THE ESTABLISHMENT OF A PERIODICAL, TO BE THE ORGAN OF THE BLACK AND COLORED RACE ON THE AMERICAN CONTINENT[64]

Your Committee, to whom was referred the duty of enquiring into the expediency of establishing a literary periodical, which should at the same time be the organ of the National Board of Commissioners,[65] would respectfully submit, that they have investigated the subject as thoroughly as the limited time allowed them would permit.

It is evident to every one that a well-conducted and well supported press, is a most potent instrument in the moral and intellectual culture, and elevation of any people. This is emphatically a reading age and country. Elaborate works, which in former ages were only within the reach of the wealthy few, by popular and cheap editions, are brought within the reach of the most humble individual, or the most limited purse. While reviews, magazines and newspapers cover the land, authors, editors, essayists and critics have become a numerous class, and by no other class, in an enlightened country, is so great an influence exerted upon the characters of their fellow men, and the future destinies of the race. Theirs is the silent influence which goes with the divine into his study, and dictates the character of the doctrines and precepts which he must impress upon the minds of his hearers; it mounts the rostrum with the orator, and paints each glowing period

64. The report was presented to the National Emigration Convention of Colored People, which met in Cleveland, 24–26 August 1854. The committee consisted of Whitfield, James T. Holly, and William Lambert of Michigan. According to the *Proceedings of the National Emigration Convention of Colored People*, prior to the convention, Whitfield "sent in" a paper on "the subject of establishing a Quarterly Repository" (17). The committee's report probably drew heavily on that paper, and it was printed in the *Proceedings* itself (28–31), which is the source of the text here.

65. The convention proposed a national leadership council consisting of nine members. As reported in the *Proceedings*, the National Board of Commissioners would be "the *first* and only *practically* useful and comprehensively intelligent organization, unselfish in its motives and designs, ever established in this country among the black inhabitants of the republic" (5).

that rolls from his tongue; it enters the halls of legislation, and gives tone to the debates, and shapes the character of the enactments; it enters the school-house, and stamps its impress upon the enquiring mind of the child, and moulds the character of the rising generation; in the domestic circle, and in every relation of life, its all-pervading influence is felt. It is this facility for the rapid spread of intelligence and communication of ideas, which principally distinguishes the civilization of the nineteenth century from all that have preceded it; and any movement which fails to secure a due share of this potent influence in its favor, will be always undervalued in public estimation. This, like all other great influences in this country, has been arrayed against the negro; and while both law and public sentiment have conspired to place him in such a position as to exclude him entirely from all the usual avenues of literature and science, and render it impossible for him to make any great proficiency in intellectual culture, the very fact that in those attainments he is inferior to the privileged class, who have every incentive to exertion, and every opportunity for improvement, is brought up as evidence of natural inferiority; thereby making the legitimate fruit of oppression the strongest argument in favor of the oppressor, and of perpetuating the oppression. In accordance with this spirit, every branch of learning has been subsidized for the express and avowed purpose of keeping the Negro down, and preventing him from ever rising in the scale of humanity. For this purpose the whole power of the government must be used to prevent the abolition of negro Slavery, or the building up of black nationality anywhere. The Word of God must be corrupted, and the evidence of the Church adduced to show that Slavery is a blessing, compatible with the exercise of the highest and purest Christianity; the well established facts of history must be falsified, and science must be suborned to prove that black is white, and that white is black; and to cap the climax, some American savans have given a practical answer to the question of the Prophet, "Can the Ethiopian change his skin?"[66] by *proving* as they say,

66. Jeremiah 13:23.

that the ancient Ethiopians belonged to the white race. But one more step is needed, and that, by the skill of American ethnologists, and the pure morals and strict virtue of American patriarch, is rendered comparatively easy, that is, to prove that the *modern* negroes, as well as the *ancient* ones, belong to the white race, and bring us back to the old-fashioned doctrine of the unity of the human species.

In spite of all the obstacles thrown in their way, many colored men in this country have made attainments in literature and science which would be creditable to any class of men, under the most favorable circumstances; but for want of a proper sphere of action, have remained unknown, except in the immediate circle of their acquaintance. There has never yet been any fair exhibition of the literary and scientific attainments of the Negro race. In the literature of the whites, as well as in white society, the negro is at a discount, and nothing can raise him in either, but occupying a manly independent position, attained by his own efforts.

There have been published in the United States some twenty different newspapers, edited and conducted, most of them with marked ability, by colored men; all of which, with the single exception of Frederick Douglass' paper, after progressing for a longer or shorter period, have been suspended for want of patronage.[67] While, therefore, your committee have nothing to offer in relation to newspapers in the country conducted entirely by colored men,[68] they would earnestly recommend the establishment of a periodical, which, while it

67. The *Aliened American*, we are assured, and requested by Mr. DAY to say, will be, and is on the eve of being resumed [Whitfield's note]. Based in Cleveland under the editorship of William Howard Day, the *Aliened American* commenced publication in April 1853 but went under in May 1854 when Day resigned the editorship because of his poor health.

68. The Committee had here recommended to the consideration of the Convention, *Frederick Douglass' paper* [*sic*], but in consequence of the illiberal and supercilious position assumed by him towards the Convention, from the issue of the Call till its assembling, denouncing those concerned as being "unintelligent," "unwise," &c., and eventually refusing to publish any thing in favor of the movement, but promptly giving publicity to every thing against it, the Convention properly declined to entertain

shall be the organ of the Board of Emigration,[69] shall be open to a fair and impartial discussion of all questions connected with the welfare, progress and development of the Negro race; and that it should also be made a literary periodical, calculated to give a fair representation of the acquirements of the colored people. That to this end, some of the ablest colored writers in both hemispheres should be engaged as its regular contributors, and articles invited on the various branches of literature, science, art, mechanics, law, commerce, philosophy, theology, et cetera; and that all the articles shall be the productions of colored men, except such selections as may be useful in illustrating some of the fundamental principles of this organization. Your committee believe that the publication of such a work would effect an incalculable amount of good in various ways. It would bring the evidences of progress before those who deny such progress, in a manner that it could not be disputed; and by furnishing manifestations of talent on the part of a large number of colored persons, would have more effect than masterly productions by one or two individuals; at the same time that it would present to colored men of ability an inducement to write, which they do not now possess.

Your committee think it should be made a standard and permanent work, capable of reflecting credit upon our race; and to this end would recommend that each number be stereotyped, so as to make it a permanent compendium and book of reference, to mark the progress and development of the race. Such a work, having a special duty to perform, should differ in some of its essential features from any of the other publications, the monthly magazines, and quarterly reviews of the day. Although we have no doubt that such a periodical can, in a very short time, be made to sustain itself, and pay a fair profit; yet to place its success beyond contingency, and to ensure its

---

the proposition of the Committee, and consequently ordered it to be struck out. COMMITTEE ON PUBLICATION [Whitfield's note]. For more on Douglass's opposition to the Cleveland emigration convention, see *Arguments, Pro and Con*, in this edition.

69. That board was conceived as part of the National Board of Commissioners.

permanency, we would recommend that all its expenses be paid from, and all its receipts go into, the regular fund of the Board. While we could not in the smallest degree slight or disparage the Anti-Slavery cause, and while such a periodical must, from its very nature, be the most powerful and efficient of all anti-Slavery instrumentalities, yet we would recommend that no piece be received merely for its anti-Slavery qualities, but only for its merit as a literary production. The fact that a considerable portion of its patrons, as well as contributors, will probably be from other countries, and that solid will doubtless predominate over light matter in its pages, together with economical reasons, show that it should be a quarterly. We, therefore, recommend for your adoption the following resolution:

Resolved, That the Board of Commissioners be authorized and instructed to establish a quarterly periodical, as the organ of this organization, (in accordance with the foregoing outline,) to be called the Africo-American Repository,[70] or some other name equally suggestive of its character.

JAMES M. WHITFIELD,

J. THEODORE HOLLY,

WM. LAMBERT.[71]

Mr. Whitfield having to leave Cleveland for Buffalo, to answer the demands of a telegraphic dispatch, the report was handed in by Mr. Holly.[72]

70. The prospectus appeared in 1856 (see the next selection), but there is no evidence that Whitfield managed to publish an issue.

71. Born free in Trenton, New Jersey, abolitionist William Lambert (ca. 1818–90) relocated to Detroit in 1838 and shortly thereafter served as secretary of the first Michigan state convention of colored citizens. He continued to play a key leadership role in the black community, contributing writings to various African American newspapers and helping fugitive slaves make their way to Canada West. In 1854 he announced his support of Delany's and Whitfield's emigrationist movement.

72. According to the *Proceedings*, Whitfield was summoned from the convention and was not able to deliver the report in person (it was presented by Holly). There is no mention of why Whitfield had to leave the convention.

PROSPECTUS OF THE AFRIC-AMERICAN QUARTERLY REPOSITORY[73]

THE NATIONAL EMIGRATION CONVENTION OF THE COLORED PEOPLE OF NORTH AMERICA, after mature and deliberate consideration, at two successive sessions, held at Cleveland Ohio, August, 1854, and again in August 1856,[74] has resolved to authorize the publication of a Quarterly Periodical devoted to the general interest of the colored people, to be called "The AFRIC-AMERICAN REPOSITORY."

It is evident to every one who comprehends the spirit of the age, that a well conducted, and well supported press, is one of the most potent instrumentalities that can be used at the present time in effecting the moral and intellectual culture, and elevation of any people. The present is emphatically a reading age. Elaborate works, which in former ages were only within the reach of the wealthy few, are now cheapened by the demand of the masses, who use these means to improve their minds and to enlighten their understanding; and thus have been popularized the acquisitions of literature and science, the once hoarded treasures of the aristocratic circle. This demand has called forth and trained up a class of authors, editors, essayists and critics, of ripe and elevated minds, who exert a powerful, but silent influence in every enlightened country. Theirs is the silent influence which goes with the divine into his study, and dictates the character of the doctrines and precepts which he must impress upon his hearers' minds;—it mounts the rostrum with the orator, and paints each glowing period that rolls from his tongue;—it enters the halls of legislation, and gives tone to the debates, and shapes the character of enact-

73. From the *Provincial Freeman and Weekly Advertiser*, 6 December 1856, 1. Edited by Mary Ann Shadd Cary in Canada West, the newspaper had adopted the emigrationist position of Whitfield and Delany, though with an emphasis on the importance of Canadian emigration as well.

74. The 1856 convention was held in Cleveland, at the A.M.E. Church, but was not as well attended as the 1854 convention. Martin Delany was unable to attend because of an illness.

ments;—it enters the school house, and stamps its impression upon the enquiring mind of the child and moulds the character of the rising generation;—in the domestic circle, and in every relation of life, its all pervading influence is felt. It is this facility for the subtle insinuation of thought, the rapid spread of intelligence and the vivid communication of ideas which principally distinguishes the civilization of the nineteenth century from that of every preceding age.

So all controlling is this influence of the press, that any movement, or any class of community that fails to wield its potent power, must always be depreciated and undervalued in the public estimation. And if this power should happen to be totally arrayed against such class or society, then dreadful indeed is the vortex in which they are engulphed.

Nevertheless, it is just such an influence that has been arrayed against the negro in this country, which has formed an unhallowed conspiracy with unjust law, and prejudicial customs of the United States, to close up from him, every avenue of political, literary, scientific or artistic advancement. Hence, whilst wicked legislation has deprived him of every inherent right and privilege of manhood in the States,—and the prejudice of social customs has excluded him from an advantageous communion with the whites in the halls of learning, and the workshops of industry; at the same time, the influence of the press has been used to point out the results of this wicked deprivation, and the effects of this prejudicial exclusion as the evidence of the negro's natural and inherent inferiority! Thus under this baneful influence, the whole power and policy of the American government has been used to prevent the abolition of negro slavery, and to discourage the up-building of a negro nationality any where. The Word of God has been corrupted, and the evidence of renegade ministers of the gospel has been adduced to show that slavery is a blessing, compatible with the exercise of the highest and purest christianity; the well established facts of ancient history have been distorted and falsified, to prove that the negro race has never been distinguished in the history of the world; and the lofty aims and the noble purposes of science have been prostituted to establish the pernicious theory that this persecuted race have ever been semi-savages, forming the connecting link between man and the brute creation.

But in spite of all these obstacles thrown in their way, many colored men in this country have made attainments in literature and science which would be creditable to any class of men, under the most favorable circumstances. Nevertheless, for want of a proper sphere of action they have remained unknown, except in the immediate circle of their acquaintance. There has never yet been a mature and fair exhibition of the literary and scientific attainments of the negro race. In the literature of the whites, as well as in white society, the negro is at a discount, and nothing can raise him in either, but occupying a manly and independent position, attained by his own efforts.

It has therefore been maturely resolved upon to enter the arena of public literature, to exhibit the intellectual capacities of the negro race, and vindicate them before the world by the publication of a periodical designed to concentrate in one brilliant focus the most cultivated intellects, and the highest order of talents that are or may yet be developed among the descendants of Africa.

For this purpose, as the enterprise shall progress, the ablest colored writers in both hemispheres will be engaged as regular contributors, on all the various branches of literature, art, science, mechanics, law, commerce, philosophy, theology, etc. Thus all the articles shall be the productions of colored men, except such selections as may be useful to illustrate the general design of the periodical. The services of eight corresponding editors, to assist the senior editor, all of this class, have already been secured.[75]

Whilst this periodical must from its fundamental nature be one of the powerful of all Anti-Slavery instrumentalities, yet it will not be

75. Among that group were Delany, James Holly, William C. Monroe, Mary Ann Shadd (Cary), and Mary E. Bibb (ca. 1820–77), a black educator and journalist who was the widow of the former slave and autobiographer Henry Bibb (1815–54). The Bibbs, who had been living in Detroit, emigrated to Canada in the early 1850s.

confined to the particular policy, neither will it be devoted to the special tenets that characterize any existing anti-slavery organization.

As this periodical is intended as a preeminent Literary work, for extended circulation both at home and abroad, and being warned by the precarious support, and ephemeral existence of numerous hebdomadal[76] issues that have been published as the organs of the negro race by isolated geniuses among us, it is determined to issue the numbers of the Afric-American Repository at periodical intervals of three months.

In order to give an intermediate opportunity to canvas and extend its circulation, the issue of the first four numbers will take place at long and irregular intervals.

The first number will be issued July 1857, for January 1858; the second number will be issued January 1858, for April of the same year; the third number will be issued in May, 1858, for the following July; and the fourth number in September, 1858, for the succeeding October. Thereafter it will be issued regularly for January, April, July and October of each year in the month preceding its date.

Each number of the periodical will contain from 160 to 200 octavo pages, and will be embellished with a fine Steel Engraving, of some distinguished negro, commencing with Faustin I, Emperor of Hayti.[77] Articles will also be published in French, contributed by Haytian authors! It will be furnished at 75 cents per number, or $3 per year to single subscribers, in the United States and Canada; and $1 per number, or $4 per year to subscribers, in the West Indies and Europe. Agents taking not less than ten copies each, to supply subscribers, will be furnished with the numbers of each issue, at a reduction of one-third from the above rates. Orders with cash remittances for the

76. Weekly.

77. Faustin-Élie Soulouque (1782–1867) was elected president of Haiti in 1847 and in 1849 declared himself Faustin I, Emperor of Hayti. Soulouque favored dark-skinned loyalists in a country in which many were of mixed race, and he was deposed in 1857.

first number must be sent by the first of April 1857, to ensure attention. Weekly, monthly or quarterly newspapers and periodicals inserting the Prospectus and the following notice three times, and sending one copy of their publication containing the insertion, to the senior Editor, will be entitled to a regular exchange. All articles for publication must be sent to the senior Editor.

Address, JAMES M. WHITFIELD, *Senior Editor, Buffalo, N.Y.*

NOTICE

ONE HUNDRED active and intelligent persons are wanted to act as Agents and Canvassers for the above Periodical, in the United States, Canada, the West Indies and Europe. Such Agents must send in their orders accompanied with the cash, and 10 or more copies will be sent to one order at 50 cents per copy in the United States and Canada; and 67 cents per copy in the West Indies and Europe. This is a discount of 33 per cent on the regular price charged single subscribers, which is made for the benefit of Agents, who will be entitled to receive 75 cents for each copy supplied to subscribers in the United States and Canada, and to receive $1 per copy from subscribers supplied in the West Indies and Europe.

Send your orders to
JAMES M. WHITFIELD, *Buffalo, N.Y.*

LINES,

ADDRESSED TO MR. AND MRS. J. T. HOLLY,
ON THE DEATH OF THEIR TWO INFANT
DAUGHTERS[78]

"Suffer little children to come unto me, and forbid
   them not: for of such is the kingdom of God."[79]
'Tis true the favored ones of Heaven
   Are called from earth in early youth,
Ere evil thoughts and deeds have given
   A will opposed to heavenly truth.

'Tis not for them the tear should fall,
   'Tis not for them the sigh should rise,
Whose infant spirits burst their thrall
   Returning to their native skies.

Weep not for them, they ne'er shall know
   The evils of this earthly life,
Which in the hearts of mortals sow
   Deception, envy, hate and strife.

Weep not for them, it is not meet
   To bend in sorrow o'er their bier;
With wails the spirit's joy to meet;
   And greet its triumph with a tear.

78. From *Frederick Douglass' Paper*, 29 February 1856, 4. At the end of the poem, Douglass prints Whitfield's place of composition and date of completion: "BUFFALO, Feb. 20th, 1856." During the mid-1850s, Whitfield had become friendly with James Theodore Holly, sharing an interest in African American emigration to the southern Americas. An ordained Episcopal priest living in New Haven at the time of the death of these daughters, Holly eventually emigrated to Haiti in 1861.

79. Matthew 19:14; Mark 10:14.

For though their infant souls are fled
   Far from their prison house of clay,
Th' immortal spirit is not dead,
   But lives in heaven's eternal day.

Oh! who would stay their upward flight,
   And draw their spirits back again
From heaven's pure and holy light,
   To this dark world of woe and pain.

Then weep not for the favored ones,
   Who tutored now in heavenly lays,
Join in with pure angelic ones
   To utter forth Jehovah's praise.

LETTER TO FRANK P. BLAIR, JR., 1 FEBRUARY 1858[80]

LETTER FROM J. M. WHITFIELD,
EDITOR OF THE AFRICAN-AMERICAN REPOSITORY,
(A COLORED MAN.)

Buffalo, New York, Feb. 1, 1858

DEAR SIR: Having read a portion of your late speech in Congress in favor of colonizing free blacks in Central or South America,[81] I have taken the liberty of addressing you, feeling, as one of that race, and an advocate of the same policy, a vital interest in its success.

In August, 1854, a Convention was held at Cleveland of those colored men in favor of emigration to the West India islands, Central and South America. That Convention organized a Board of Emigration, which appointed a commissioner (Rev. J. T. Holly, now rector of St. Luke's church, New Haven) to go to Hayti, and confer with the Haytien government upon the subject.[82]

80. From the appendix to Frank P. Blair Jr., *The Destiny of the Races of this Continent: An Address Delivered before the Mercantile Library Association, Boston, Massachusetts. On the 26th of January 1859* (Washington, D.C.: Buell & Blanchard, Printers, 1859), 37–38. Also included in the appendix are supportive letters from Holly and Delany. Because both Holly's and Whitfield's letters were reprinted in Carter G. Woodson's pioneering *The Mind of the Negro as Reflected in Letters Written During the Crisis, 1800–1860* (1926), with Whitfield's letter immediately following Holly's, the letter to Blair has been misidentified as a letter to Holly in several Whitfield bibliographies.

81. On 14 January 1858, Francis (Frank) P. Blair Jr. (1821–75), a U.S. representative from Missouri, gave a speech before Congress calling for financial support for his plan to encourage the free blacks to emigrate to what he called in his 1859 *The Destiny of the Races of this Continent* "the vacant regions of Central and South America" (23). A graduate of Princeton University, Blair practiced law in his home state of Kentucky before moving to Missouri. Following two terms in the Missouri legislature, Blair became the lone Free-Soiler in Congress from a slave state when he was elected in 1856. He urged southerners to adopt a policy of continued emancipation by deportation and colonization and opposed the extension of slavery on economic as well as social and moral grounds. A veteran of the Mexican-American war, Blair distinguished himself during the Civil War as a general in the Union army.

82. Holly first visited Haiti in 1855. He moved there in 1861, and in 1878 he was named bishop of the Orthodox Apostolic Church of Haiti.

That Government expressed itself ready to offer the most liberal inducements to emigrants, and to grant them every assistance in its power. It was also intended to send a commissioner to the British islands, New Granada, and the Central American States, but for lack of pecuniary means were unable to do so. And here, allow me to say, is one of the curses of our condition in this country: we are all so miserably poor that we are unable to help each other, and so scattered that it is impossible to have union of action even where there is perfect unanimity of sentiment; so that while there are hundreds—yes, thousands—of enterprising and industrious colored men, ready and anxious to embark immediately in any feasible movement of emigration to either of the places named, the means to commence such a movement properly are not attainable among them. * * *[83]

The Colonization Society removes to Africa a few hundreds yearly, at an expense which, if judiciously applied according to the practical principles developed by Mr. Thayer in his organized system of Kansas emigration,[84] would plant twice as many *thousands* in Central America, with everything requisite for their rapid progress; and the true interest of both the white and black races seems to require such a policy.

The fact is, the Saxon and negro are the only positive races on this continent, and the two are destined to absorb into themselves all the others; and, like two positive poles, they repel each other; and if the one is destined to occupy all the temperate regions of this hemisphere, it is equally certain that the other will predominate within the tropics. The Slavery propagandists unwittingly admit the same, when they declare negro labor to be indispensable in those regions. The question which suggests itself to the intelligent mind is, shall things be permit-

---

83. The asterisks in the body of the text perhaps indicate cuts from a longer letter.

84. In 1854, Eli Thayer (1819–99), an educator from Massachusetts, formed the Massachusetts Emigrant Society, which funded the "emigration" of antislavery settlers to the Kansas Territory. The society merged with the New York Emigrant Aid Company in 1855. Thayer was elected to the U.S. House of Representatives in 1857.

ted and encouraged to reach their natural developments, which no combination of circumstances can prevent, (however much it may retard it,) by the peaceful influence of free labor? or shall the Slavery propagandists be allowed to interfere and check for a time the march of civilization, when the ultimate result must be to usher in, through war and anarchy, the very same state of things, which might have been much sooner and easier reached by peaceful and legitimate means, to the great benefit of the whole civilized world? You have answered the question in a manner which indicates the far-seeing statesman as well as the noble-hearted philanthropist, and I sincerely hope that a majority of Congress may be induced to adopt the same just and liberal policy.

Respectfully, yours,

J. M. WHITFIELD

LETTER TO THE *PACIFIC APPEAL*, 2 AUGUST 1862[85]

MR. EDITOR — "Put down the rebellion at all hazards!" is the cry of the Governors and people of the loyal States; but there is one hazardous step yet to be taken, which would help the work wonderfully. There have been many killed and much money spent, but the fighting has only passed from one white American's hands to that of another, and yet the rebellion is not put down. The U.S. Government must make an alliance with her own people, i.e. the people of color to help

85. From the 9 August 1862 issue of the *Pacific Appeal* (p. 2), an African American newspaper established in 1862 and edited by Philip A. Bell (1808–89). Whitfield wrote his letter from Marysville, a thriving gold-rush town approximately 120 miles northeast of San Francisco. During the same month that Whitfield published this letter, the War Department authorized General Rufus Saxton to form the Union army's first black regiment, the First South Carolina Volunteers. The Union army began actively recruiting black troops shortly after Lincoln's Emancipation Proclamation of 1 January 1863.

to do it. Also, abrogate or nullify the odious Dred Scott decision,[86] which takes from every colored man his rights as a man and a citizen; and if that is not enough to make him a man, in common with other men, make a law that will open the ranks to him, according to merit, and let there be no slavery under the stars and stripes. Let this be done, and you have my word for it, the President of the United States will soon stand at the head of the greatest and most valiant army the world ever saw, or perhaps ever will see again.

J. M. W.
Marysville, Aug. 2, 1862

86. In 1857 the Supreme Court ruled in the case of *Dred Scott v. Sandford* that African Americans could never become citizens of the United States and that blacks, in the words of Chief Justice Roger Taney (1777–1864), were "so far inferior, that they had no rights which the white man was bound to respect."

PART III Poems from California

In a letter published in the 25 November 1853 issue of *Frederick Doug-lass' Paper*, and then reprinted in *Arguments, Pro and Con, on the Call for a National Emigration Convention*, Whitfield states that the first essay he had ever written for publication, back in the winter of 1838–39, was "on the subject of emigration, recommending a concentration upon the borders of the United States, having particular reference to California."[1] As Whitfield elaborates in the letter, he wanted African Americans to emigrate to California before "white men have gone in and possessed the soil, and made laws to degrade the negro below the level of the brute." The fact that Whitfield chose to move there with his family in late 1861 or early 1862 suggests that he believed there were still opportunities for African Americans in the state. If he had traveled South of the U.S. border sometime between 1859 and 1861, he now wanted to lay claim to his rights as a U.S. citizen. Whitfield quickly found a place in San Francisco's African American community as a political leader, Prince Hall Mason and eventual Grand Master, barber, and poet. He did not publish many poems during this period, but he was called upon at key moments to offer commemorative verse on public occasions.

All of Whitfield's California poetry appeared in either the *Pacific Appeal* or the *Elevator*, two of the most prominent African American newspapers in northern California. Subtitled "A Weekly Journal, de-voted to the Interests of the People of Color," the *Pacific Appeal* was published by Peter Anderson in San Francisco, with Philip A. Bell act-ing as editor.[2] "A Weekly Paper," wrote Bell, "is needed in California as much as in the Atlantic States: one which will be the exponent of our views and principles, our defense against calumny and oppression, and our representative among one of the recognized institutions of Civilization." The *Pacific Appeal* was dedicated to advocating equality before the law for African Americans and, in particular, repealing the laws that prohibited blacks from testifying in court cases in which a white person was a party. In the 5 April 1862 inaugural issue of the newspaper, Bell appealed to California's black population: "There are said to be six thousand Colored people in California, sufficient, if only one tenth subscribe, to support our paper; that proportion, say six hundred, we must have within six months, for the remaining four hundred, we must depend on our neighbors on the northern coast."[3] If we take the paper's sales agents as indicative of demographics, the *Pacific Appeal* points to the growing presence of African Americans throughout the West. The paper had agents in a number of towns between San Francisco and the eastern border of California in its early months, and by 1864 it had agents as far north as Victoria, British Columbia, and as far south as Panama.

A four-page weekly, the *Pacific Appeal* would have been an ideal venue for Whitfield, since it regularly featured poetry in a dedicated column. In the issue of 9 August 1862, which published Whitfield's letter on the need for the Union to recruit black troops, the editors announced "with pride and pleasure" that Whitfield had agreed to become a contributing editor. And yet he failed to publish there on a regular basis, perhaps because of a recurring health problem. As Whitfield remarked in a letter of 22 October 1862 to the newspaper: "I have had a kind of inflammation in the eyes which has prevented me from contributing to the columns of the APPEAL. I will try and make a commencement in a few days, and endeavor to be more prompt in the future." Whitfield ultimately published just two poems and two letters in the newspaper, or at least in the extant issues of the paper. The editors no doubt hoped for more from Whitfield, for in the issue of 14 March 1863 there was yet another announcement that "J. M. Whitfield" had been added to the roster of "Our Contributors."[4]

Whitfield's first poem for the *Pacific Appeal*, "Elegy on T. T. Tatum, Esq.," appeared in November 1862, in the midst of the Civil War, and lamented the death of Thomas T. Tatum, an African American abolitionist whom Whitfield knew during the early 1840s in Buffalo. Making use of seven ballad stanzas in iambic tetrameter, Whitfield characterizes Tatum as a solider who "died in harness on the field," taking "freedom for his battle-word, / Truth for his sword, and faith his shield." In "Elegy," Whitfield interpreted the Civil War very differently from Whitman, who in *Drum-Taps* (1865) presented the war as a fight among white brothers. Whitfield's reminder that African American activists had long soldiered in the battlefield of political discourse, and were now prepared to soldier in war, anticipates several poems in Melville's *Battle-Pieces and Aspects of the War* (1866). In "The March to Sea" and "The Swamp Angel," for example, Melville, in the way of African American poets like Whitfield and Albery Allson Whitman, underscores the importance of blacks' military participation to the successful outcome of the Civil War.

Whitfield's only other poem for the *Pacific Appeal* was thematically different from his Tatum elegy and, in fact, departed from all of his poetry during this era in that it did not address the topic of freedom or slavery. In "To A—. Sketching from Nature," published in May 1863, Whitfield's speaker encourages the anonymous subject to continue honing her artistic skills by imitating the perfection of nature. With its emphasis on aesthetics, "To A—." is akin to poems in *America* such as "To S. A. T." and "Ode to Music."

Whitfield's final three poems were brought out under the auspices of the *San Francisco Elevator*, a black periodical founded by Bell after he resigned from the *Pacific Appeal*. Beyond what it indicates about a possible disagreement between Bell and his former employer, Peter Anderson, the appearance of the *Elevator* suggests that the black community in northern California was large enough to support two periodicals. Taking "Equality Before the Law" as the motto for the paper, Bell was keen to emphasize that the weekly would advocate civil liberties: "Such are our general principles and objects, but we will have, in addition thereto, a special mission to fulfill; we will labor for the civil and political enfranchisement of the Colored people—not as a distinct and separate race, but as American citizens."[5] Although Whitfield published more poems while living on the East Coast, his California pieces commemorating African American and national history signaled his continuing presence as a public poet.

In January 1867, Whitfield published in the *Elevator* "A Poem, Written for the Celebration of the Fourth Anniversary of President Lincoln's Emancipation Proclamation"—a 400-line poem in iambic tetrameter surveying the history of the country from its beginnings. Whitfield enumerates, in the vein of one of Whitman's catalogs, a litany of regional, national, and international identities that comprise the United States and worked to preserve the Union and abolish slavery. The poem reveals Whitfield's familiarity with Norse mythology and the Book of Joshua and his keen understanding of the Civil War as a global event. Rather than depicting emancipation as simply the liberating of America's black subjects, Whitfield illustrates how the Emancipation Proclamation liberated the country writ large, freeing the very spirit of liberty from a far-reaching slaveocracy that had held it in bondage. In contrast to his position less than a decade earlier on the value of black emigration, Whitfield's message and tone here are distinctly more patriotic, a difference in perspective due as much perhaps to being on the other side of the Civil War as to being on the far western side of the country.

Whitfield's "Celebration of the Fourth Anniversary" differs markedly from a work like Whittier's "The Proclamation" (1863), which used the occasion of Lincoln's Emancipation Proclamation to cast former slaves as allegorical St. Patricks who had thrown off the yokes of their master Milcho, a Druidical priest. Whereas for Whittier the Emancipation Proclamation heralded the emergence of the United States as a Christian nation, for Whitfield it heralded the emergence of a democratic nation. For Frances Harper, who also wrote a poem on the subject, "President Lincoln's Proclamation of Freedom" (1871), the Emancipation Proclamation promised to change the landscape of America:

It shall flush the mountain ranges;
And the valleys shall grow bright;
It shall bathe the hills in radiance,
And crown their brows with light.[6]

Along with Ezra R. Johnson's "Emancipation Oration," Whitfield's "Celebration of the Fourth Anniversary" was initially delivered before approximately 2,000 whites and blacks crowded into Platt's Hall in San Francisco on 1 January 1867. Dedicated to the Brannan Guards, the first "organized military company of colored men in California," Johnson's speech emphasized the active participation of African Americans as agents in the efforts to eradicate slavery, taking special notice of black military men. "We gave twenty thousand precious lives of our race to save the life of the nation. We now demand of the government a fulfillment of its pledge. We will labor incessantly until we obtain all the rights and privileges that are enjoyed by the Caucasian race."[7] Both Johnson's oration and Whitfield's poem were enthusiastically received, and the lecturer and the poet published their works together as a small volume that included notices from five different newspapers praising them. Typical of these encomiums was a review from the *Bulletin* that noted that "the poem of J. M. Whitfield was well delivered, and a worthy production," and that both the "orator and poet were frequently interrupted with applause." The occasion even got national attention from the *Christian Recorder*, with a writer for the journal remarking that the "colored people of San Francisco, Cal., had a monster celebration of the Anniversary of the Birth Day of Freedom, on the first of January. . . . An oration was delivered by Dr. Ezra R. Johnson, formerly of New Bedford, Mass., also a poem by Mr. James M. Whitfield, who, it is acknowledged, gives evidence of the highest order of poetic genius. . . . We have received in pamphlet form a copy of the oration and poem handsomely printed at the office of our colored contemporary The Elevator, a spirited journal, which is doing wonders in the golden state to promote our elevation."[8]

Whitfield's next poem for the *Elevator*, "Poem, Written . . . for the Celebration of the Anniversary of West Indian Emancipation . . . ," appeared in August 1868 and was almost identical to his earlier "Stanzas for the First of August." The poem had recently been read at Hayes (Valley) Park by William Ector in what was apparently a public commemoration organized by San Francisco's black community. Beyond a few alterations in punctuation, tenses, and words, Whitfield added a completely new final stanza. Whereas the first published version is composed of six sestets, the latter version concludes with an additional octave. If the earlier version conveyed the anger that many African Americans felt about the United States, then the *Elevator* version neutralized that sentiment. Instead of having the poem punctuated with the final line that the British West Indies alone were "freedom's home," the revised version welcomes an emancipatory future for nations throughout the world.

While Whitfield's "Celebration of the Fourth Anniversary" outlined the history of the United States from its founding to Lincoln's decree, his last published poem presented an image of freedom that correlated liberation with the "natural" march of historical progress. Published in May 1870, Whitfield's "Poem" was composed in rhymed couplets and occasional quatrains and opens with a quotation from Homer's *Odyssey*. Appearing during the early years of Reconstruction, "Poem" offers the hope that the postslavery United States could finally fulfill its destiny to become a "city upon a hill"—a model for the rest of the world to emulate. At the heart of the poem, however, are darker images of power and evil reminiscent of "The Vision":

> And all along the stream of Time,
> In every age, in every clime,
> Have proud oppression's altars stood,
> Forever drenched with human blood,
> Where right is sacrificed to wrong,
> The feeble offered to the strong.

Whitfield would die less than a year later, with his buoyant but ultimately haunting final poem in some ways foreseeing the failure of Reconstruction.

NOTES

1. We have located the "Resolutions" from the Cleveland convention of 1838 but not this particular essay; see "Resolutions of the People of Cleveland, on the Subject of African Colonization," *Colored American*, 2 March 1839, 1.

2. Bell was one of the most prominent newspaper figures of the nineteenth century, having worked with Charles B. Ray on the *Colored American* in the late 1830s and early 1840s. For more on the history of African American periodicals in California, see I. Garland Penn, *The Afro-American Press and Its Editors* (Springfield, Mass.: Wiley & Co. Publishers, 1891); Armistead S. Pride and Clint C. Wilson II, *A History of the Black Press* (Washington, D.C.: Howard University Press, 1997); and Ivy G. Wilson, "Periodicals, Print Culture, and African American Poetry," in *A Companion to African American Literature*, ed. Gene Andrew Jarrett (Malden, Mass.: Wiley-Blackwell, 2010). On northern California, and specifically San Francisco, during the years when Whitfield resided in the region, see Douglas Henry Daniels, *Pioneer Urbanites: A Social and Cultural History of Black San Francisco* (Berkeley: University of California Press, 1991), 12–17. On African Americans' migrations to California, see Rudolph M. Lapp, *Blacks in Gold Rush California* (New Haven: Yale University Press, 1995), and Lawrence B. De Graaf, Kevin Mulroy, and Quintard Taylor, eds. *Seeking El Dorado: African Americans in California* (Seattle: University of Washington Press, 2001).

3. *Pacific Appeal*, 5 April 1862, 2.

4. *Pacific Appeal*, 9 August 1862, 2; 1 November 1862, 2; 14 March 1863, 2.

5. *San Francisco Elevator*, 6 December 1867, 1.

6. Frances Harper, "President Lincoln's Proclamation of Freedom," in *A Brighter Coming Day: A Frances Ellen Watkins Harper Reader*, ed. Frances Smith Foster (New York: Feminist Press, 1990), 186.

7. *Emancipation Oration, by Dr. Ezra R. Johnson, and Poem, by James M. Whitfield, Delivered at Platt's Hall, January 1, 1867, in Honor of the Fourth Anniversary of President Lincoln's Proclamation of Emancipation* (San Francisco: Elevator Office, 1867), 10. According to an article from the *Pacific Appeal* on the unpaginated frontispiece, "The hall was densely crowded with two thousand white and colored persons indiscriminately."

8. Ibid.; "Matters in General," *Christian Recorder*, 9 February 1867, 1.

ELEGY ON T. T. TATEM, ESQ.[1]

A HERO's soul has passed away,
    Gone to a higher, brighter sphere;
His body to its kindred clay
    Is borne, and leaves us sorrowing here.

He was a hero, not like those
    Whose sanguine path o'er field and flood
Is marked by heaps of slaughtered foes,
    And traced in characters of blood.

But his the soul that dared to stand
    Alone in conflict for the right,
With all the powers of the land
    Arrayed against him in the fight,

With freedom for his battle-word,
    Truth for his sword, and faith his shield,
He fought the battles of the Lord,
    And died in harness on the field.

Why should we sorrow? Not that he
    Is called from labor to reward,
To share the glorious destiny
    That waits true servants of the Lord.

---

1. From the *Pacific Appeal*, 15 November 1862, 4. In all probability the elegy is for Thomas T. Tatum, an African American abolitionist and barber whom Whitfield knew from Buffalo. According to the *Colored American*, Tatum and Whitfield attended a number of meetings together in the early 1840s, including the "GREAT MEETING IN BUFFALO" at which African Americans initiated a campaign for voting rights. Whitfield and Tatum served on the "committee of five" charged to "procure signatures to the petition" (*Colored American*, 9 January 1841, 2).

'Tis sweet when men of sterling worth
   Are summoned to their final doom,
That those who wrought with them on earth
   Should bear their bodies to the tomb,

And there deplore the loss of those
   Who led the vanguard of the fight,
And overthrew the banded foe,
   Of virtue, freedom, truth and right.

TO A—. SKETCHING FROM NATURE[2]

YES, priestess at the shrine of Art,
   Continue still to sketch from Nature;
And let her charms inspire thy heart
   To be her humble imitator.
Her flocks and herds, her plains and hills,
   Her bright cascades, her sunny fountains,
Her babbling brooks, her gentle rills,
   Her dark ravines, her towering mountains,
Her cataracts, her placid lakes,
   The gentle stream, the boundless ocean,
Which on the shore in thunder breaks,
   When tempests set the waves in motion;
The clouds which deck the sunset sky,
   With varying hues arrayed before you,
Whose brilliant tins attract the eye,
   And dazzle with their blaze of glory,—
Require a hand well trained by Art,
   To trace their grandeur, grace and beauty,
May it be thine to fill the part,
   And thus perform a pleasing duty.

2. From the *Pacific Appeal*, 23 May 1863, 4.

A POEM,

WRITTEN FOR THE CELEBRATION OF THE
FOURTH ANNIVERSARY OF PRESIDENT
LINCOLN'S EMANCIPATION PROCLAMATION[3]

To P. A. Bell, Esq.,[4]
a pioneer in the intellectual elevation of his race,
these lines are respectfully inscribed by the author.

More than two centuries have passed
   Since, holding on their stormy way,
Before the furious wintry blast,
   Upon a dark December day,
Two sails, with different intent,
   Approached the Western Continent.[5]

---

3. From *Emancipation Oration, by Dr. Ezra R. Johnson, and Poem, by James M. Whitfield, Delivered at Platt's Hall, January 1, 1867, in Honor of the Fourth Anniversary of President Lincoln's Proclamation of Emancipation* (San Francisco: Elevator Office, 1867), 23–32. As described in the pamphlet, "During the delivery of the Oration and Poem the speakers were frequently interrupted by loud bursts of applause" (32).

Although Abraham Lincoln's Emancipation Proclamation (1 January 1863) granting freedom to slaves was specifically directed at the Confederate States of America as a wartime measure, it was regarded by many African Americans as the bold action that laid the groundwork for the prohibition of slavery in the Thirteenth Amendment, which was ratified on 18 December 1865.

4. Philip Alexander Bell (1808–89) was one of the most prominent African American journalists of the nineteenth century. He established his first newspaper, the *Weekly Advocate*, in New York City in 1837. He moved to San Francisco in 1860, and by 1862 he had become an editor of the *Pacific Appeal*, one of the first black newspapers in California. In 1865 he established his own newspaper, the *Elevator*, which was devoted to the cause of gaining all the rights of citizenship for African Americans.

5. For a similar historical reflection, see William Wells Brown's *Clotel* (1853), the first novel published by an African American. In chapter 21, Brown refers to two sails arriving in North America on the same day around December 1820: the freedom-loving Pilgrims at Plymouth Rock in Massachusetts and the English slave traders with their first cargo of slaves at Jamestown, Virginia.

One vessel bore as rich a freight
   As ever yet has crossed the wave;
The living germs to form a State
   That knows no master, owns no slave.
She bore the pilgrims to that strand
   Which since is rendered classic soil,
Where all the honors of the land
   May reach the hardy sons of toil.
The other bore the baleful seeds
   Of future fratricidal strife,
The germ of dark and bloody deeds,
   Which prey upon a nation's life.
The trafficker in human souls
   Had gathered up and chained his prey,
And stood prepared to call the rolls,
   When, anchored in Virginia's Bay—
   His captives landed on her soil,
   Doomed without recompense to toil,
   Should spread abroad such deadly blight,
   That the deep gloom of mental night
   Spreading its darkness o'er the land,
   And paralizing every hand
   Raised in defense of Liberty,
   Should throw the chains of slavery
   O'er thought and limb, and mind and soul,
   And bend them all to its control.
   New England's cold and sterile land
   Gave shelter to the pilgrim band;
   Virginia's rich and fertile soil
   Received the dusky sons of toil.
The one bore men whose lives were passed
   In fierce contests for liberty—
Men who had struggled to the last
   'Gainst every form of tyranny.

Vanquished in many a bloody fight,
    Yet still in spirit unsubdued;
Though crushed by overwhelming might,
    With love of freedom still imbued,
They bore unto their Western home,
    The same ideas which drove them forth,
As houseless fugitives to roam
    In endless exile o'er the earth.
And, on New England's sterile shore,
    Those few and feeble germs took root,
To after generations bore
    Abundance of the glorious fruit —
    Freedom of thought, and of the pen,
    Free schools, free speech, free soil, free men.
    Thus in that world beyond the seas,
    Found by the daring Genoese,[6]
    More than two centuries ago
    A sower wandered forth to sow.
He planted deep the grains of wheat,
    That generations yet unborn,
When e'er they came to reap and eat,
    Might bless the hand that gave the corn;
    And find it yield that priceless bread
    With which the starving soul is fed;
    The food which fills the hungry mind,
    Gives mental growth to human kind,
    And nerves the sinews of the free
    To strike for Truth and Liberty.
Yet, planted at the self-same time
    Was other seed by different hands,

6. Christopher Columbus (ca. 1451–1506).

To propagate the deadliest crime
   That ever swept o'er guilty lands —
   The crime of human slavery,
   With all its want and misery —
   The harrowing scenes of woe and pain,
   Which follow in its ghastly train.
The same old feud that cursed the earth
   Through all the ages of the past,
In this new world obtained new birth,
   And built again its walls of caste,
More high and deep, more broad and strong,
   On ancient prejudice and wrong.
The same old strife of every age,
   Inherited by son from sire,
Which darkens each historic page,
   And sends a discord through the lyre.
   Every bard, who frames his song
   In praise of Freedom, Truth, and Right,
Rebukes the gathered hosts of wrong,
   And spreads the rays of Freedom's light —
   That strife, long fought in Eastern lands,
   Was transferred to the Western strand.
   The same old seeds of endless strife,
   Deep in the Nation's inmost life
   Were sown, to yield in after years
   A plenteous crop of blood and tears.
'Twas here the dragon's teeth were sown,
   And crops of armed men sprang up;
Here the Republic, mighty grown,
   Drank deep rebellion's bitter cup;
Here, where her founders sowed the wind,
   They reaped the whirlwind's furious blast —
Proudly refusing to rescind
   The deadly errors of the past,

They drew the sword, by deed and word
   To rivet slavery's bloody chain,
And, slaughtered by th' avenging sword,
   Their bones strew many a battle plain.
   The strife of aristocracy
   In conflict with democracy,
   Was here renewed, with greater zeal,
   And danger to the common weal.
One century and a half had flown
   When Freedom gained the first great fight;
Defied the power of the throne,
   And bravely proved the people's might,
     When banded in a righteous cause,
   To overthrow oppressive laws.
'Twas then, when struggling at its birth,
   To take its proper place beside
The other Nations of the earth,
   The rule of justice was applied;
   And all mankind declared to be
   Inheritors of Liberty;
   With right to make their freedom known,
   By choosing rulers of their own.
But when it came t' enforce the right,
   Gained on the well-contested field,
Slavery's dark intrigues won the fight,
   And made victorious Freedom yield;
   Giving each place of power and trust,
   To those who, groveling in the dust,
   Seek to extend the giant crime
   Of Slavery through all coming time.
   The victory won at fearful cost,
   Over a mighty monarch's host,
   By which oppression's power seem'd foiled
     On the Atlantic's western shore,

And those who through long years had toiled,
 The burden of the battle bore,
In order that this land might be
A home and refuge for the free,
Were doomed to see their labor lost—
Their victory won at fearful cost,
Over oppression's mighty power,
Surrendered in the trying hour;
And made to strengthen slavery's hand,
Ruling with iron rod the land.
The power the warrior's hand had lost,
 The politician's skill restored;
And slavery's votaries could boast
 Intrigue was mightier than the sword.
But fraud and force in vain combined
To check the progress of the mind;
And every effort proved in vain
T' enslave the cultivated brain.
The same ideas the pilgrims brought
 When first they crossed the wintry wave,
Spreading throughout the land were fraught
 With light and freedom to the slave:
And hence where slavery bore the rule,
It labored to suppress the school,
Muzzle the tongue, the press, the pen,
As means by which the rights of men
Might be discussed, and Freedom's light
Break up the gloom of slavery's night.
Efforts which, in a better cause
 Had brought their authors deathless fame,
Were made to frame oppressive laws,
 And to arouse, excite, inflame,
The vilest passions of the throng,
 And stir that bitter prejudice

Which makes men blind to right and wrong,
    And opens wide that deep abyss
Where pride of rank, and caste, and race,
    Have left such marks of bitter hate,
As nought but time can e'er efface,
    To foment discord in the State.
    But vain their efforts to control
    The aspirations of the soul;
For still a faithful few were found
    Who would not bend the servile knee,
But in each conflict stood their ground,
    And boldly struck for Liberty.
From year to year the contest grew,
    Till slavery, glorying in her strength,
Again war's bloody falchion[7] drew,
    And sluggish freedom, roused at length,
Waked from her stupor, seized the shield,
And called her followers to the field.
And at that call they thronging came,
With arms of strength, and hearts on flame;
Answering the nation's call to arms,
The northern hive poured forth its swarms;
The lumbermen of Maine threw down
    The axe, and seized the bayonet;
The Bay State's[8] sons from every town,
    Left loom and anvil, forge and net;
The Granite State[9] sent forth its sons,
    With hearts as steadfast as her rocks;
The stern Vermonters took their guns,
    And left to others' care their flocks;

7. A single-edged sword.
8. Massachusetts.
9. New Hampshire.

Rhode Island and Connecticut
　　Helped to fill up New England's roll,
And showed the pilgrim spirit yet
　　Could animate the Yankee soul.
　　The Empire State[10] sent forth a host,
　　　　Such as might seal an empire's fate;
　　Even New Jersey held her post,
　　　　And proved herself a Union State.
　　The Key-Stone[11] of the Union arch
　　　　Sent forth an army true and tried;
Ohio joined the Union march,
　　And added to the Nation's side
　　A force three hundred thousand strong,
　　While Michigan took up the song;
　　Wisconsin also, like the lakes,
　　When the autumnal gale awakes,
　　And rolls its surges on the shore,
　　Poured forth its sons to battle's roar.
　　The gallant State of Illinois
　　Sent forth in swarms its warlike boys.
　　On Indiana's teeming plain,
　　Thick as the sheaves of ripened grain,
　　Were soldiers hurrying to the wars
　　To battle for the Stripes and Stars.
From Iowa fresh numbers came,
　　While Minnesota joined the tide,
And Kansas helped to spread the flame,
　　And carry o'er the border side
　　The torch the ruffians once applied
　　When fiercely, but in vain, they tried

10. New York.
11. Pennsylvania.

The people of their rights to spoil,
And fasten slavery on her soil.
From East unto remotest West,
From every portion of the North,
The true, the bravest, and the best,
Forsook their homes and sallied forth;
And men from every foreign land
Were also reckoned in that band.
The Scandinavians swelled the train,
The brave Norwegian, Swede, and Dane,
And struck as though Thor[12] rained his blows
Upon the heads of haughty foes;
Or Odin's[13] self had sought the field
To make all opposition yield.
Italia's sons, who once had cried
Loud for united Italy,
And struck by Garibaldi's[14] side
For union and equality—
Obtained another chance to fight
For nationality and right.
The Germans came, a sturdy throng,
And to the bleeding country brought
Friends of the right, foes of the wrong,
Heroes in action as in thought,
Sigel, and Schurz,[15] and many others,
Whose names shall live among the brave,

12. God of thunder in Germanic and Norse mythology.

13. God of war, and the chief god of Germanic and Norse mythology.

14. The Italian revolutionary Giuseppe Garibaldi (1807–82) was a key figure of the Risorgimento, the literary and ideological movement that helped to liberate the Italian states from foreign domination and united them politically under the House of Savoy.

15. Franz Sigal (1824–1902) was a German military officer and immigrant who participated in both the republican revolutions of 1848 in Europe and in the Civil War;

Till all men are acknowledged brothers,
   Without a master or a slave.
Ireland's sons, as usual, came
   To battle strife with shouts of joy,
With Meagher and Corcoran[16] won such fame
   As well might rival Fontenoy.[17]
Briton and Frank, for centuries foes,
   Forgot their struggles, veiled their scars,
To deal on slavery's head their blows,
   Fighting beneath the Stripes and Stars.
From the Atlantic's stormy coast,
   Unto the broad Pacific's strand,
Came pouring forth a martial host,
   From every portion of the land.
They came, as flocking sea birds swarm,
   Whene'er the cloud-king mounts his throne
And calls the warriors of the storm
   To sweep the earth from zone to zone.
They came as come the rushing waves
   When o'er the sea the tempest raves.
They came as storm clouds quickly fly
   When lightnings flash along the sky,
   And on the Southern plains afar

---

he came to be regarded as one of the most visible symbols of immigrant support for the Union cause. Like Sigal, the German-born Carl Schurz (1829–1906) also participated in the German Revolution of 1848 and in the Civil War, taking an antislavery position in his support of the Union.

16. Irish nationalist Thomas Francis Meagher (1823–67) fought for Ireland's independence from England; after he emigrated to the United States, he fought in the Union army. Michael Corcoran (1827–63) was an Irish American brigadier general and friend of Lincoln who led the 69th Regiment into the First Battle of Bull Run.

17. In the Battle of Fontenoy of 11 May 1745, the French defeated the allied Anglo-Dutch-Hanoverian forces in the War of Austrian Succession. The Irish brigade fought on behalf of the French.

Soon burst the thunderbolts of war.
In quick and fierce succession fell
The furious showers of shot and shell.
Though East, and West, and North combined,
    And foreigners from every land
With all that art and skill could find,
    They could not crush the rebel band.
They clung unto th' accursed thing,
    That which they knew accursed of God,
Nor strength, nor skill could victory bring
    With that accursed thing abroad.
When Abraham,[18] the poor man's friend,
    Assumed the power to break the chain.
Obey the Lord, and put an end
    To slavery's dark and bloody reign,
To make the nation shield from harm
    Its loyal sons of every hue,
In its defence receive and arm
    All those who to its flag were true,
He found the touchstone of success,
For then Jehovah deigned to bless,
And smile upon the nation's arms,
And give it rest from war's alarms.
Thus men of every land and tongue,
    Of every station, every hue,
Were found the Union hosts among,
    Enlisted with the boys in blue;
And all mankind should freely draw
    The prize for which their lives were given;
"Equality before the law,"[19]
    To every person under heaven.

18. Abraham Lincoln (1809–65), the sixteenth president of the United States.
19. The motto of Philip Bell's newspaper, the *Elevator*.

As storms and tempests pass away,
   And leave the sun's enlivening light,
Our war-cloud brought the opening day
   To slavery's long and gloomy night.
As storms and thunder help to clear
And purify the atmosphere,
E'en so the thunders of the war,
Driving malaria afar,
Have purged the moral atmosphere,
And made the dawn of freedom clear.
From swamps and marshes left undrained
   Malarious vapors will arise,
From human passions, unrestrained,
   Rise fogs to cloud our moral skies:
So now, from portions of the land
   Where lately slavery reigned supreme,
Its conquered chiefs together band,
   Concocting many an artful scheme,
By which Oppression's tottering throne
   May be restored to pristine power,
And those who now its rule disown
   Be made submissive to its power.
The self-styled Moses brings the aid
   Of power and place to help them through,
To crush the race by him betrayed,
   And every man who, loyal, true,
   And faithful to his country's laws—
   Declines to aid the tyrant's cause.
Our real Moses, stretched his rod
   Four years ago across the sea,
And through its blood-dyed waves we trod
   The path that leads to Liberty.
His was the fiery column's light,
   That through the desert showed the way,

Out of oppression's gloomy night,
    Toward the light of Freedom's day;
And, like his prototype of old,
    Who used his power, as Heaven had told,
    To God and to the people true,
    Died with the promised land in view.
And we may well deplore his loss,
    For never was a ruler given,
More free from taint of sinful dross,
    To any Nation under Heaven.
And ever while the earth remains,
    His name among the first shall stand
Who freed four million slaves from chains,
    And saved thereby his native land.
Though Achans[20] rise within the camp,
    And covet slavery's cursed spoil,
Invent oppressive laws, to cramp
    The energies of men who toil
Through hardship, danger, sickness, health,
To add unto the Nation's wealth—
Some Joshua[21] shall yet arise,
    Whose hand shall extirpate the seeds
Sown by this worst of tyrannies,
    Which ripen into bloody deeds
Such fiendish murders as of late
    Occur in every rebel State.
While Freedom falters, once again
    The fogs and mists begin to rise,

20. According to the book of Joshua, Achan was stoned to death by the Israelites for having stolen consecrated metals and contributing to the fall of Jericho through his selfishness (Joshua 7:1).

21. Succeeding Moses, who had led the Hebrew slaves out of Egypt and across the Red Sea, Joshua led the Israelites across the Jordan River (Joshua 3–4).

And cast their shadows o'er the plain,
 Vailing the issue from our eyes,
On which the nation yet must stand, —
Impartial freedom through the land.
Yet once again our moral air
 Is tainted by that poisonous breath,
Which Freedom's lungs can never bear,
 Which surely ends in moral death.
Then let the people in their might
 Arise, and send the fiat forth,
That every man shall have the right
 To rank according to his worth;
That north and south, and west and east,
All, from the greatest to the least,
Who rally to the nation's cause,
Shall have the shield of equal laws,
Wipe out the errors of the past,
Nursed by the barbarous pride of caste,
And o'er the nation's wide domain,
Where once was heard the clanking chain,
And timorous bondmen crouched in fear,
Before the brutal overseer,
Proclaim the truth that equal laws
Can best sustain the righteous cause;
And let this nation henceforth be
In truth the country of the free.

POEM,

WRITTEN BY J. M. WHITFIELD FOR THE
CELEBRATION OF THE ANNIVERSARY
OF WEST INDIAN EMANCIPATION, AT
HAYES PARK, AUGUST 3D, 1868[22]

From bright West Indies' sunny seas
Comes borne upon the balmy breeze
The joyous shout, the gladsome tone,
Long in those bloody isles unknown, —
Bearing across the heaving wave
The song of the unfettered slave.

No charging squadrons shook the ground
    When freedom here her claims sustained;
No cannon with tremendous sound
    The noble patriots' cause maintained; —
No furious battle-charger neighed,
No brother fell by brother's blade.

None of those desperate scenes of strife,
    Which marked the warrior's proud career —
The awful waste of human life —
    Have ever been enacted here:
But truth and justice came from heaven,
And slavery's galling chain was riven.

---

22. From the *San Francisco Elevator*, 14 August 1868, 1. According to the *Elevator*, Whitfield was not in attendance at Hayes Park, in San Francisco, and the poem was read by William Ector. The poem celebrates the thirty-fourth anniversary of the emancipation of all slaves in the British Empire on 1 August 1834.

'Twas moral force which broke the chain
    That bound eight hundred thousand men;
And when we see it snapped in twain,
    Shall we not join in praises then?—
And prayers unto Almighty God,
Who smote to earth the tyrant's rod?

And from those Islands of the sea,
    The scenes of blood, and crime, and wrong—
The glorious anthem of the free
    Now swells in mighty chorus strong;
And tells the oppressed, where'er they roam,
Those Islands now are freedom's home.

Hasten, O Lord! the glorious time,
    When every where beneath the skies—
From every land and every clime,
    All to equality and justice rise;
When the bright sun of liberty
    Shall shine on each despotic land,
And all mankind, from bondage free,
    Adore the wonders of Thy hand.

POEM[23]

"God fixed it certain that whatever day,
Sees man a slave takes half his worth away."[24]

Thus sang the bard, and yet how long,
    Eternal God of life and light,
The weak have cowered beneath the strong,
    And might usurped the place of right.
Where history's dawning rays begin
    To permeate tradition's shade,
We find the ties of race and kin
    By avaricious greed betrayed,
And feeble brothers bought and sold
To satiate the thirst for gold;
And all along the stream of Time,
In every age, in every clime,
Have proud oppression's altars stood,
Forever drenched with human blood,
Where right is sacrificed to wrong,
The feeble offered to the strong.
The mitred priest and sceptred king,
Their rigid creeds and edicts bring,
And bind the human mind in chains,
To guard their palaces and fanes;
And trembling hosts with fear obey,
The bigot's and the despot's sway.
Class legislation still remains,
    The fruitful cause of civil strife;

---

23. From the *San Francisco Elevator*, 6 May 1870, 3.

24. From Homer's *Odyssey*, and cited by Thomas Jefferson in his *Notes on the State of Virginia* (1787), Whitfield's probable source. Jefferson refers to this passage in Query 14 just before stating, "I advance it, therefore, as a suspicion only, that the blacks, whether originally a distinct race, or made distinct by time and circumstances, are inferior to the whites in the endowments both of body and mind."

And every country's statutes stains,
    With blots that sap a nation's life.
Through every age has heard the cry
Of zealous shouts for liberty,
And marked some peoples rend in twain
The links of their oppressor's chain,
And step into the foremost place,
Among the freest of the race—
Yet all in vain the song arose
For Freedom's triumph o'er her foes;
In vain has Freedom's praise been sung
By men of every land and tongue,
For those who just had rent the chains
    From off their own long fettered limbs,
Still pouring forth in joyful strains,
    Proud Freedom's thrilling battle hymns,
Have been among the first to tread
    Down in the dust a weaker brother,
Their own and neighbor's blood to shed
    To bind the chain upon each other,
And prove their right to freedom's prize,
    By showing power to tyrannize.

The Greeks adored at Freedom's shrine;
Sages and bards with theme sublime,
And thoughts that seemed almost divine,
In stirring prose and polished rhyme
Rehearse the mighty deeds of those
Who triumphed over Freedom's foes,
And watered with their blood the tree
Which bore the fruit of liberty—
While all around their bondmen stood,
Their brethren of a kindred blood,
And wrung their fettered hands to see

Such mockery made of liberty.
The Roman also loud proclaimed
　　The people's voice the voice of God:
Then, of such conduct not ashamed,
　　Smote all the earth beneath his rod;
Princes and peasants dragged in chains
　　Yoked captive monarchs to his car,
Presented at his gorgeous fanes,
　　As lawful trophies of the war,
A bloody death to myriad braves,
And living death to million slaves.

The golden rule in Christian lands
Brought aid to Freedom's just demands:
But spite of churches, spite of schools,
In spite of Christian creeds and rules,
Despotic sway and feudal power,
Have ruled unto the present hour—
Till Christendom, like heathen lands,
Obeys the tyrant's proud commands,
And never daring to complain,
Accepts the despot's iron reins.

One favored land at last is found
　　Where pride of rank, and caste, and place,
Whose galling chains so long have bound
　　The upward progress of the race
Is broken, and true freedom reigns
O'er all the Union's wide domains—
Freedom to think and speak the truth,
　　Though tyrants' vassals cringe and cower;
Freedom to train the mind of youth,
　　Unawed by superstition's power;
Freedom of each to think and feel,
　　And spread his uttered thoughts abroad,

To labor for the common weal,
   Responsible to none but God.
Freedom of speech and of the pen;
Free schools, free press, free soil, free men.
The principles, the pilgrims brought—
   When from their native country driven,
On rude New England's coast they sought
   And found the long desired haven—
As fruitful germs of living truth,
Were planted in the minds of youth,
Were planted deep in generous hearts,
   And we behold the growing tree
O'erspread the land till all its parts
   Rest in the shade of liberty.
Those living germs of truth and right,
   Sown in the infant nation's mind,
Have served to curb oppression's might,
   And break at last the chains which bind
The mind to superstitious rite,
The body to a master's might.
Though many years of bitter strife
   Have rent the land from sea to sea,
Emerging to a higher life
   Of order, law and liberty,
She takes her station in the van,
Foremost of all the race of man.
In every art that tends to grace
Or elevate the human race;
She stands the first by land and wave,
Without a master or a slave.
Her area o'er a surface spread,
   Where all the climes of earth are found,
Where gifts from every land are shed
   In prodigal profusion round,

While north and south from zone to zone,
   And east and west, from sea to sea,
Is heard the soul-entrancing tone
   Which guides the march of liberty.
Where once the lowly slave-hut stood,
Springs up the freeman's proud abode;
Where slave-pens marked the trader's rule,
Grows up at once the church and school,
Her commerce covering every sea
   And every spot where man is found,
Bears forth the banner of the free
   The habitable earth around:
And he who sees its folds ascend
   As if to meet the morning sun,
Or views it gracefully descend
   At booming of the evening gun,
Has felt that ne'er was seen so fair
   A symbol of a land so free,
And breathes within himself a prayer
   That hers may be the destiny
To lead the van of Freedom's march,
   Till on the earth there shall remain,
Nowhere beneath the heaven's blue arch
   A single slave to clank his chain;
Till all around, from east to west,
   From north to south, on land and sea,
Like us, the nations shall be blest
   With equal laws and liberty.

Selected Bibliography

Bell, Howard H. "The Negro Emigration Movement, 1849–1854: A Phase of Negro Nationalism." *Phylon* 20 (1959): 132–42.

Brawley, Benjamin. *Early Negro American Writers: Selections with Biographical and Critical Introductions.* Chapel Hill: University of North Carolina Press, 1935.

Brown, Lois. *Pauline Elizabeth Hopkins: Black Daughter of the Revolution.* Chapel Hill: University of North Carolina Press, 2008.

Brown, Sterling. *The Negro in American Fiction: Negro Poetry and Drama.* 1937. New York: Arno Press, 1969.

Brown, William Wells. *The Black Man: His Antecedents, His Genius, and His Achievements.* Boston: James Redpath, Publisher, 1863.

Bruce, Dickson D., Jr. *The Origins of African American Literature, 1680–1865.* Charlottesville: University of Virginia Press, 2001.

De Graaf, Lawrence B., Kevin Mulroy, and Quintard Taylor, eds. *Seeking El Dorado: African Americans in California.* Seattle: University of Washington Press, 2001.

Delany, Martin Robison. *The Condition, Elevation, Emigration and Destiny of the Colored People of the United States.* Philadelphia: published by the author, 1852.

Fordham, Monroe. *A History of Bethel A.M.E. Church, Buffalo, New York, 1831–1977.* Buffalo: Bethel History Society, 1978.

Goldman, Mark. *High Hopes: The Rise and Decline of Buffalo, New York.* Albany: State University of New York Press, 1983.

Harding, Jennifer Riddle. "Gagged Petitions and Unanswered Prayers: James M. Whitfield's Anxious America." *CLA Journal* 47 (2003): 175–92.

Hill, James L. "James Monroe Whitfield." In *African American Authors,*

1745–1945: A Bio-Bibliographical Critical Sourcebook, edited by Emmanuel S. Nelson, 474–78. Westport, Conn.: Greenwood, 2000.

Jackson, Blyden. *A History of Afro-American Literature*. Vol. 1. Baton Rouge: Louisiana State University Press, 1989.

Laryea, Doris Lucas. "James Monroe Whitfield." In *Dictionary of Literary Biography*, vol. 50, *Afro-American Writers before the Harlem Renaissance*, edited by Trudier Harris, 260–63. Detroit: Gale, 1986.

Leonard, Keith D. *Fettered Genius: The African American Bardic Poet from Slavery to Civil Rights*. Charlottesville: University of Virginia Press, 2006.

Levine, Robert S. *Martin Delany, Frederick Douglass, and the Politics of Representative Identity*. Chapel Hill: University of North Carolina Press, 1997.

———, ed. *Martin R. Delany: A Documentary Reader*. Chapel Hill: University of North Carolina Press, 2003.

Loggins, Vernon. *The Negro Author: His Development in America to 1900*. New York: Columbia University Press, 1931; Port Washington, N.Y.: Kennikat Press, 1964.

Miller, Floyd J. *The Search for a Black Nationality: Black Emigration and Colonization, 1787–1863*. Urbana: University of Illinois Press, 1975.

Pease, Jane H., and William H. Pease. *They Who Would Be Free: Blacks' Search for Freedom, 1830–1861*. Urbana: University of Illinois Press, 1990.

Peterson, Carla L. "Commemorative Ceremonies and Invented Traditions: History, Memory, and Modernity in the 'New Negro' Novel of the Nadir." In *Post-Bellum, Pre-Harlem: African American Literature and Culture, 1877–1919*, edited by Barbara McCaskill and Caroline Gebhard, 34–56. New York: New York University Press, 2006.

Redmond, Eugene. *Drumvoices: The Mission of Afro-American Poetry*. Garden City, N.Y.: Anchor, 1976.

Robinson, William H., ed. *Early Black American Poets: Selections with Biographical and Critical Introductions*. Dubuque, Iowa: W. C. Brown Co., 1969.

Sherman, Joan R., ed. *African-American Poetry of the Nineteenth Century: An Anthology*. Urbana: University of Illinois Press, 1992.

———. *Invisible Poets: Afro-Americans of the Nineteenth Century*. Urbana: University of Illinois Press, 1989.

———. "James Monroe Whitfield, Poet and Emigrationist: A Voice of Protest and Despair." *Journal of Negro History* 57 (1972): 169–76.

Wagner, Jean. *Black Poets of the United States: From Paul Laurence Dunbar to Langston Hughes*. Urbana: University of Illinois Press, 1973.

Whitley, Edward. *American Bards: Walt Whitman and Other Unlikely Candidates for National Poet*. Chapel Hill: University of North Carolina Press, 2010.

Wilson, Ivy G. "Periodicals, Print Culture, and African American Poetry." In *A Companion to African American Literature*, edited by Gene Andrew Jarrett, 133–48. Malden, Mass.: Wiley-Blackwell, 2010.

MIX
Paper from
responsible sources
FSC® C013483
FSC
www.fsc.org